Unlocking the Mysteries of Praise

Unlocking the Mysteries of Praise

SECOND EDITION

Doris J Sanders

D.J. SANDERS MINISTRIES LLC
MILWAUKEE

Published by:
D. J. Sanders Ministries LLC
P.O. Box 090725
Milwaukee, WI 53209

First edition published 2011. Second edition 2014

ISBN –13: 978-0-9836341-0-2
ISBN –10: 0983634106
Edited by David Yost

Printed by CreateSpace, An Amazon.com Company

Contents

Preface

As I sat in the midst of a Christian church service, I heard, saw, and felt the praises lifted up toward God. I thought to myself, if everybody can praise and worship God like these people, this world would change in a most positive way. Then I remembered a verse from the Holy Bible. It says, "For God *is* the King of all the earth: sing ye praises with understanding" (Psalm 47:7). To understand is to grasp the significance or importance of an issue, in this case praise. In addition, understanding is like taking a key and unlocking a door to see what is on the other side. On the other side of the door are dots, or elements of praise, that need to be connected in order to see a complete, developed clear picture. The Holy Bible describes the word *understanding* as follows:

> Happy *is* the man *that* findeth wisdom, and the man *that* getteth understanding. For the merchandise of it [understanding] *is* better than the merchandise of silver, and the gain thereof than fine gold. She *is* more precious than rubies: and all the things thou canst desire are not to be compared unto her. Length of days *is* in her right hand; *and* in her left hand riches and honour. Her ways *are* ways of pleasantness, and all her paths *are* peace. She *is* a tree of life to them that lay hold upon her: and happy *is every one* that retaineth her. (Proverbs 3:13-18)

Being wise, one shows a "marked deep understanding, keen discernment, and a capacity for sound judgment": it will bring about blessings. What is a blessing? The word bless is defined as "a special favor, mercy, or benefit," that a person receives not because of their merits or virtues. What blessing will one receive with understanding praise? Now, I am wonder, do all people who praise God really understand these dots or elements of praise that they are displaying toward Him? This book looks through the pages of the Holy Bible, Christian tapes, books, and dictionaries seeking the keys to unlock the mysteries of the elements of praise. The subject of praise is complex, yet very rewarding. Once a person learns these mysteries of praise, then they can "Sing ye praises with understanding" (Psalm 47:7) and receive the blessing it yields.

Doris Jean Sanders
Milwaukee, WI
June 2008

Introduction

This book takes us through a journey searching the Holy Bible, seeking God's wisdom on praise. Praise is a tool—or better yet, a weapon—that God has given His children to battle against negative forces in this life. In this world, there is a struggle going on, and the human race is the chess pieces displayed on the battlefield. In Ephesians 6:10-12 it reads,

> Finally, my brethren, be strong in the Lord, and in the power of his might. Put on the whole armour of God, that ye may be able to stand against the wiles of the devil. For we wrestle not against flesh and blood, but against principalities, against powers, against the rulers of the darkness of this world, against spiritual wickedness in high *places*.

Here is a secret that many people do not know: every person has a right to choose on which side of the war one will serve. There is no middle ground. If you think that a middle ground exists, then you have fallen for a trick of the enemy keeping you from the blessings of God. The Old Testament records God giving this option to humanity, but every person has a right to choose for oneself. It reads,

> See, I have set before thee this day life and good, and death and evil; In that I command thee this day to love the LORD thy God, to walk in his ways, and to keep his commandments and his statutes and his judgments, that thou mayest live and multiply: and the LORD thy God shall bless thee in the land whither thou goest to possess it. But if thine heart turn away, so that thou wilt not hear, but shalt be drawn away, and worship other gods, and serve them; I denounce unto you this day, that ye shall surely perish,

> *and that* ye shall not prolong *your* days upon the land, whither thou passest over Jordan to go to possess it. I call heaven and earth to record this day against you, *that* I have set before you life and death, blessing and cursing: therefore choose life, that both thou and thy seed may live: That thou mayest love the LORD thy God, *and* that thou mayest obey his voice, and that thou mayest cleave unto him: for he *is* thy life, and the length of thy days: that thou mayest dwell in the land which the LORD sware unto thy fathers, to Abraham, to Isaac, and to Jacob, to give them. (Deuteronomy 30:15-20)

The New Testament confirms that humanity has a choice in their future.

> For there is no difference between the Jew and the Greek: for the same Lord over all is rich unto all that call upon him. For whosoever shall call upon the name of the Lord shall be saved. (Romans 10:12, 13)

In a war, a soldier can only take orders from one captain. In this spiritual warfare, the two captains are God the creator and Satan the fallen angel. Jesus talks about this in Matthew 6:24, "No man can serve two masters: for either he will hate the one, and love the other; or else he will hold to the one, and despise the other. Ye cannot serve God and mammon." There is no middle ground in the war zone.

Having the right to choose is a blessing in itself. When Adam sinned, all of humanity received the sentence of spiritual death. The Bible states that all of humanity was under the control and ruled by the Devil because of sin. Satan and his host are not in Hell yet. Their headquarters is located in the heavenly realms, the atmosphere. Satan is known as "the prince of the power of the air" (Ephesians 2:2).

> And you *hath he quickened*, who were dead in trespasses and sins: Wherein in time past ye walked according to the course of this world, according to the prince of the power of the air, the spirit that now worketh in the children of disobedience. (Ephesians 2:1, 2)

However, through Jesus Christ, humanity has a right to choose life. 1 Corinthians 15:22 reads, "For as in Adam all die, even so in Christ shall all be made alive." The second "all" applies only to believers, people who chose God the creator. Believers have weapons to fight this spiritual warfare against the Devil's schemes, rulers, authorities, power of this dark world, and the spiritual forces of evil in the heavenly realms. Satan's army is well-organized and evil.

The only way a human being can fight a spiritual being is through obedience to God the creator and the Word of God. What is the Word of God? The Word of God is a weapon, a sword that is used in combat against one's enemy. There are seven characteristics of the sword of God. First, the sword of God is His Word. In the Holy Bible, from Genesis to Revelation, God has set His standard to every phase in life that man can and will encounter. It is the responsibility of the believer to find the passage of scripture to solve their problems. Second, the sword is a weapon—a spiritual righteous force—that is used in combat to kill the enemy's spiritual strongholds. Third, the sword is living, which means that it is sufficient to handle the job at hand now. Fourth, the sword is active. Active means that the sword is producing something, a result will occur when it is used. Fifth, "For the word of God *is* quick, and powerful, and sharper than any two-edged sword, piercing even to the dividing asunder of soul and spirit, and of the joints and marrow, and *is* a discerner of the thoughts and intents of the heart" (Hebrews 4:12). The sword of God is more powerful than the enemy sword and devices that he swings your way. Sixth, the sword of God cuts up satanic schemes and plots. Seventh, the sword of God judges between right and wrong. The judge can tell the enemy what to do. When a person passes a judgment, that judgment is communicated by a spoken word released in the atmosphere.

In Proverbs 18:21, it reveals the power of the tongue. "Death and life *are* in the power of the tongue: and they that love it shall eat the fruit thereof." A spoken word is released in the atmosphere. A spoken Word of God and/or praise can put to death the schemes and plots of the Devil in the life of the praiser. Praise is a positive energy that is released into the atmosphere to counteract the negative energy of the Devil. Praise is the Word of God in song. In the Word of God, it says: "For God is the King of all the earth: sing ye praises with understanding" (Psalm 47:7). That is what we are about to do, unlock and understand the mysteries of praise. We will review the element of praise from Genesis to Revelation and receive its blessings.

Chapter One

The Basics of Praise

In chapter one, we will start to build a solid foundation in understanding praise. A foundation is a "basics, principle, upon which something stands or is supported." It is very important that Christians build a solid base in order to establish unmovable faith. In chapter one some very basic questions will be answered. These questions include the following: What is praise? Why give praise to God? What is good? Who, when, and where should we praise God?

What is Praise?

In order to understand praise a definition is required. The word praise has several meanings as follow:

>   Praise is—"the act of expressing approval or admiration"
>   Praise is—"the offering of grateful homage in words or song"
>   Praise is—"to sing someone's praise"
>   Praise is—"to give praise to someone publicly and enthusiastically"
>   Praise is—'it is a physical and vocal expression of our sincere appreciation to God for all of the wonderful blessing He has provided"
>   Praise is—"to speak well of"
>   Praise is—"to applaud (clap, cheer for)"
>   Praise is—"to compliment (honor, respects)"
>   Praise is—"to extol (celebrate, adore)"

We will use the fifth definition as our working definition when we refer to the word praise. It covers all the basics of praise. Praise "is a physical and vocal expression of our sincere appreciation to God for all of the wonderful blessing He has provided."

Praise is an action word; it is something that a person has to do for him or herself, voluntarily. Praise is personal, which produces personal satisfaction. If a person will not open their mouth to release praise, clap their hands enthusiastically, dance and jump for joy in the Lord, or kneel in admiration with their own legs, they will not receive the blessing that happens during the praise experience.

Praise is like being at a banquet. People are eating, but some people are just watching and encouraging the eaters to eat more until they are full. The people who are eating will leave full and content. Those who are on the sidelines will leave empty and hungry. The food was available for all to partake. The only thing they had to do was to open up their own mouths and eat. Praise is the same way. Praise is like the law of reciprocity—you get back what you put out. The dictionary says that reciprocity "is a mutual exchange."

Why Give Praise to God?

There are countless reasons why people should give praises to God. Some reasons are very personal. However, we will discuss only eight universal reasons for praising God. It applies to everybody who calls Jesus Christ the Lord of their lives. Each of their reasons for praising God is equally important; they are directly from the Holy Bible.

As Christians, we believe that God is the creator of everything. Chapter one of the book of Genesis goes into detail about God's wonderful works. Here are a few verses from the Bible that are related to the creation of humanity. God has made humanity in His own image with authority over all the other living things on earth.

Reason #1 God is our Creator

> And God said, Let us make man in our image, after our likeness: and let them have dominion over the fish of the sea, and over the fowl of the air, and over the cattle, and over all the earth, and over every creeping thing that creepeth upon the earth. So God created man in his *own* image, in the image of God created he him; male and female created he them. (Genesis 1:26, 27)

> I will praise thee; for I am fearfully *and* wonderfully made: marvellous *are* thy works; and *that* my soul knoweth right well. My substance was not hid from thee, when I was made in secret, *and* curiously wrought in the lowest parts of the earth. Thine eyes did see my substance, yet being unperfect; and in thy book all *my members* were written, *which* in continuance were fashioned, when *as yet there was* none of them. (Psalm 139:14-16)

The power and glory that God has set upon humanity is great. God has given Christians power, joy, and a future.

Reason #2 God gives us power over demons, but most of all, God gives us joy: our name written in the Book of Life

> And the seventy returned again with joy, saying, Lord, even the devils are subject unto us through thy name. And he said unto them, I beheld Satan as lightning fall from heaven. Behold, I give unto you power to tread on serpents and scorpions, and over all the power of the enemy: and nothing shall by any means hurt you. Notwithstanding in this rejoice not, that the spirits are subject unto you; but

rather rejoice, because your names are written in heaven. (Luke 10:17-20)

And I saw the dead, small and great, stand before God; and the books were opened: and another book was opened, which is *the book* of life: and the dead were judged out of those things which were written in the books, according to their works . . . And whosoever was not found written in the book of life was cast into the lake of fire. (Revelation 20:12, 15)

As a loving Father, God gives all of humanity the same opportunities in life. People may start in life on different levels because of their parents' situations. However, God's promise is equal opportunity to everyone who will part take of His Word.

Reason # 3 God treats us all the same

Then Peter opened *his* mouth, and said, Of a truth I perceive that God is no respecter of persons: But in every nation he that feareth him, and worketh righteousness, is accepted with him. (Acts 10:34, 35)

For the LORD your God *is* God of gods, and Lord of lords, a great God, a mighty, and a terrible, which regardeth not persons, nor taketh reward: (Deuteronomy 10:17).

Throughout the Bible, God describes Himself in many different ways. For example, He told Moses to tell the children of Israel that, "I AM THAT I AM" (Exodus 3:14) God is portrayed as a healer, provider, peace, and a way maker. That is why reason number four for praising God is that nothing is impossible for God.

Reason # 4 Nothing is Impossible for God

> But our God *is* in the heavens: he hath done whatsoever he hath pleased. (Psalm 115:3)

> And Jesus came and spake unto them, saying, All power is given unto me in heaven and in earth. (Matthew 28:18)

> For with God nothing shall be impossible. (Luke 1:37)

God is aware that man is not perfect yet. His understanding, love, and patience with humanity go beyond man's understanding.

Reason #5 Praise God for His mercy and longsuffering with our sins

> The LORD *is* merciful and gracious, slow to anger, and plenteous in mercy. He will not always chide: neither will he keep *his anger* for ever. He hath not dealt with us after our sins; nor rewarded us according to our iniquities. For as the heaven is high above the earth, *so* great is his mercy toward them that fear him. As far as the east is from the west, *so* far hath he removed our transgressions from us. Like as a father pitieth *his* children, *so* the LORD pitieth them that fear him. For he knoweth our frame; he remembereth that we *are* dust. *As for* man, his days *are* as grass: as a flower of the field, so he flourisheth. (Psalm 103:8-14)

A good Father instructs and educates his children on life. God's Word (Holy Bible) is the instruction manual for all Christians. This book has history, law, instruction, poetry, songs, wisdom, prophecy, and the way to salvation all in one book. God's plans for His children's education are to be well rounded.

Reason #6 Praise God for His Word

The Word of God, the Holy Bible, tells us what is right and what is wrong according to God's standards. It cuts impurity out of one's life when obedience occurs. This is how the process works: first, they hear or read the word of God. Second, they believe what they have heard or read. That is called "faith." Third, they repent or react upon what they have heard or read. This is when God's process of healing has just awakened in that area of their life. Obedience to God's word causes a washing process to be activated in their life. Why do we need washing? All of humanity was born into sin. When Adam sinned, all of humanity was pronounced guilty. However, the Word of God has resolved this issue. In addition, Jesus has prayed for his followers' sanctification by the word of truth.

> Husbands, love your wives, even as Christ also loved the church, and gave himself for it; That he might sanctify and cleanse it with the washing of water by the word, That he might present it to himself a glorious church, not having spot, or wrinkle, or any such thing; but that it should be holy and without blemish. (Ephesians 5:25-27)

> Sanctify them through thy truth: thy word is truth… Neither pray I for these alone, but for them also which shall believe on me through their word; That they all may be one; as thou, Father, *art* in me, and I in thee, that they also may be one in us: that the world may believe that thou hast sent me. (John 17:17, 20, 21)

Reason #7 Praise God that our temptation will not overtake us

> There hath no temptation taken you but such as is common to man: but God *is* faithful, who will not suffer you to

be tempted above that ye are able; but will with the temptation also make a way to escape, that ye may be able to
bear *it*. (1 Corinthians 10:13)

That means everything that comes your way, you can handle.
Strength and character are being developed. Temptation is like testing
a person's spiritual strength. One should avoid or depart from the present of the temptation. God has never set up his children to fail. It does
not feel good to going through trials and problems, but it is better to go
through than being stuck in the midst of it. To go through something
means that steps or progress is happening while going forward. In the
growing process, one must move, but there are times one must stand
still.

Reason #8 Praise God for He is good

O give thanks unto the LORD; for *he is* good: because his
mercy *endureth* for ever. (Psalm 118:1)

This topic, God's goodness, is so big and important. This entire
next section is devoted to explaining the goodness of God. Now do
not be confused. Being good does not mean being dumb and stupid.
People are rewarded automatically for the behaviors they display. In
other words, do not purposely sin because you can ask for forgiveness.
Granted, one will receive the forgiveness, but an automatic punishment
will occur.

What is good?

During praise and worship services, people are always saying these
words, "God is good all the time, all the time God is good." What is good?
A detailed investigation on the word "good" was conducted, by using
a children and college dictionary. God's characteristic is connecting to

each definition to the word good directly from the Bible. We will prove to ourselves that God indeed is good. Because of God's goodness, He is worthy to be praised.

1. Good—a "high quality"

> For my thoughts *are* not your thoughts, neither *are* your ways my ways, saith the LORD. For *as* the heavens are higher than the earth, so are my ways higher than your ways, and my thoughts than your thoughts. (Isaiah 55:8, 9)

2. Good—"not bad"

> But whoso hearkeneth unto me shall dwell safely, and shall be quiet from fear of evil. (Proverbs 1:33)

3. Good—"not poor" (financially sound)

> The silver *is* mine, and the gold *is* mine, saith the LORD of hosts. (Haggai 2:8)

4. Good—"kindness or pleasant" (God is a gentleman—a polite being)

> Behold, I stand at the door, and knock: if any man hear my voice, and open the door, I will come in to him, and will sup with him, and he with me. To him that overcometh will I grant to sit with me in my throne, even as I also overcame, and am set down with my Father in his throne. (Revelation 3:20, 21)

5. Good—"giving help or/and advantage"

> But I *am* poor and needy; *yet* the Lord thinketh upon me: thou *art* my help and my deliverer; make no tarrying, O my God. (Psalm 40:17)

> Give us help from trouble: for vain *is* the help of man. Through God we shall do valiantly: for he *it is that* shall tread down our enemies.
> (Psalm 60:11, 12)

> Our help *is* in the name of the LORD, who made heaven and earth. (Psalm 124:8)

6. Good—"behaving properly"

> Withhold not good from them to whom it is due, when it is in the power of thine hand to do *it*. (Proverbs 3:27)

7. Good—"safe and correct, reliable, dependable"

> Counsel *is* mine, and sound wisdom: I *am* understanding; I have strength. (Proverbs 8:14)

> For I *am* the LORD, I change not; therefore ye sons of Jacob are not consumed. (Malachi 3:6)

> I will both lay me down in peace, and sleep: for thou, LORD, only makest me dwell in safety. (Psalm 4:8)

8. Good—"real, true, and genuine"

> Every word of God *is* pure: he *is* a shield unto them that put their trust in him. (Proverbs 30:5)

9. Good—"kindness" (loving-kindness)

> Have mercy upon me, O God, according to thy lovingkindness: according unto the multitude of thy tender mercies blot out my transgressions. (Psalm 51:1)

> Thus saith the LORD, Let not the wise *man* glory in his wisdom, neither let the mighty *man* glory in his might, let not the rich *man* glory in his riches: But let him that glorieth glory in this, that he understandeth and knoweth me, that I *am* the LORD which exercise lovingkindness, judgment, and righteousness, in the earth: for in these *things* I delight, saith the LORD. (Jeremiah 9:23, 24)

10. Good—"honesty"

> In hope of eternal life, which God, that cannot lie, promised before the world began. (Titus 1:2)

11. Good—"morally excellent, righteous"

> Seven times a day do I praise thee because of thy righteous judgments.
> (Psalm 119:164)

12. Good—"right and proper"

> The statutes of the LORD *are* right, rejoicing the heart: the command- ment of the LORD *is* pure, enlightening the eyes. (Psalm 19:8)

> For the word of the LORD *is* right; and all his works *are done* in truth. He loveth righteousness and judgment: the earth is full of the goodness of the LORD. (Psalm 33:4, 5)

> I know, O LORD, that thy judgments *are* right, and *that* thou in faith- fulness hast afflicted me. Let, I pray thee, thy merciful kindness be for my comfort, according to thy word unto thy servant. (Psalm 119:75, 76)

13. Good—"honorable or worthy"

> And when he had taken the book, the four beasts and four *and* twenty elders fell down before the Lamb, having every one of them harps, and golden vials full of odours, which are the prayers of saints. And they sung a new song, say- ing, Thou art worthy to take the book, and to open the seals thereof: for thou wast slain, and hast redeemed us to God by thy blood out of every kindred, and tongue, and people, and nation; And hast made us unto our God kings and priests: and we shall reign on the earth. And I beheld, and I heard the voice of many angels round about the throne and the beasts and the elders: and the number of them was ten thousand times ten thousand, and thou- sands of thousands; Saying with a loud voice,

Worthy is the Lamb that was slain to receive power, and riches, and wisdom, and strength, and honour, and glory, and blessing.

And every creature which is in heaven, and on the earth, and under the earth, and such as are in the sea, and all that are in them, heard I saying,

Blessing, and honour, and glory, and power, *be* unto him that sitteth upon the throne, and unto the Lamb for ever and ever.

And the four beasts said, Amen. And the four *and* twenty elders fell down and worshipped him that liveth for ever and ever. (Revelation 5:8-14)

14.Good—"educated and refined"

For the LORD giveth wisdom: out of his mouth *cometh* knowledge and understanding. (Proverbs 2:6)

15.Good—"free of distress or pain: comfortable"

Thou wilt keep *him* in perfect peace, *whose* mind *is* stayed *on thee*: because he trusteth in thee. (Isaiah 26:3)

Be careful for nothing; but in every thing by prayer and supplication with thanksgiving let your requests be made known unto God. And the peace of God, which passeth all understanding, shall keep your hearts and minds through Christ Jesus. (Philippians 4:6, 7)

For God hath not given us the spirit of fear; but of power, and of love, and of a sound mind. (2 Timothy 1:7)

For now on when people say, "God is good all the time, all the time God is good," think on these definitions and give God praise. Nobody deserves praise like God because He is truly good all the time.

Who, When, Where Should We Praise the Lord?

The subject of praise is huge. Its boundaries are never-ending. In this section, A. J. and Joyce Gill (1995) have posed some questions and given the scriptures to prove the answers. Use this section as a personal Bible study time with your family.

Who should praise the Lord?

All flesh	Psalm 145:21b
Kings and People	Psalm 148:11-13
My soul	Psalm 103:1, 2
Servants of God	Psalm 113:1
Everything with breath	Psalm 150:6
All His Angels	Psalm 148:2
The Saints	Psalm 145:10
All Nature	Psalm 148:7-10
The Redeemed	Psalm 107:1, 2

When are we to praise the Lord?

From morning to night	Psalm 113:3
Continually	Psalm 34:1
All day	Psalm 71:8
When downcast	Psalm 42:11
While we live	Psalm 146:2
Always	Ephesians 5:20

Where are we to praise the Lord?

In the congregation	Psalm 22:22, 25
	Psalm 107:32
	Psalm 149:1
In the sanctuary	Psalm 150:1
Everywhere	I Timothy 2:8
Among the Nations	Psalm 57:9
In His courts	Psalm 100:4
Among the multitudes	Psalm 109:30

In conclusion, chapter one has answered the basic questions and form a foundation for understands praise. As a working definition we will use, praise "is a physical and vocal expression of our sincere appreciation to God for all of the wonderful blessing He has provided." Chapter one has proven why God desires praise with eight universal reasons:

1. God is the creator of all things.
2. God give us power over demons, but most of all, God gives us joy: our name written in the Book of Life.
3. God shows no favoritism.
4. Nothing is impossible for God.
5. God's mercy and longsuffering with our sins.
6. His Word—educated, clean, and destroys the enemy.
7. God does not let temptation be stronger than our faith.
8. God is good all the time.

We have even established by whom, when and where God should be praised. A Christian's struggle is spiritual in nature; therefore, many spiritual weapons were given. Praise is a good spiritual weapon to use in one's life. We are able to go forth with understanding praise now that a foundation is in place.

Chapter Two

Seven Key Words to the Mysteries of Praise

What is a key? A key is "something that solves or explains" something else. These keys are used to open one's understanding to why various acts of praise produce blessings. A key is something that people use willingly to take them to a place they want to go. These seven keys in action will take a believer into the presence of God. These seven key words are translated in the Holy Bible as praise, but in the Hebrew language, they are Hallelujah, Yadah, Barak, Tehillah, Zamar, Towdah, and Shabach. Each one of these words offers the worshiper a deeper connection to God. Chapter two examines these seven words, and points out their biblical examples, and shows one how to operate them.

> O clap your hands, all ye people; Shout unto God with the voice of triumph. For the LORD most High is terrible [Awesome]; He is a great King over all the earth. He shall subdue the people under us, And the nations under our feet. He shall choose our inheritance for us, The excellency of Jacob whom he loved. Selah. God is gone up with a shout, The LORD with the sound of a trumpet. Sing praises to God, sing praises: Sing praises unto our King, sing praises. For God is the King of all the earth: Sing ye praises with understanding. (Psalm 47:1-7)

Understanding praise is very important. It deepens the relationship between the giver and the receiver. Understanding praise allows this connection to be strong and meaningful. Praise occurs on Sunday morning and on Bible study nights. For some believers, praise is a lifestyle. God did not set people free to be quiet. Deliverance comes with some instruction. Psalm 107:1, 2 tells us to speak of the goodness of the Lord.

> O give thanks unto the LORD, for *he is* good: for his mercy *endureth* for ever. Let the redeemed of the LORD say *so*, whom he hath redeemed from the hand of the enemy.

The enemy is Satan and his evil heavenly host. When Adam sinned, all of humanity was placed under the hand of the enemy. The word "redeems" means "to buy back." The price of a Christian is Jesus Christ's blood (Galatians 3:13, 14 and Revelation 5:9). Praise and worship is not only for us to demonstrate our love toward God while we are here on earth; it will also be going on in heaven. In the book of Revelation, there is a preview of what is to come.

> After this I looked, and, behold, a door *was* opened in heaven: and the first voice which I heard *was* as it were of a trumpet talking with me; which said, Come up hither, and I will show thee things which must be hereafter. And immediately I was in the spirit; and, behold, a throne was set in heaven, and *one* sat on the throne.... And the four beasts had each of them six wings about *him*; and *they were* full of eyes within: and they rest not day and night, saying, Holy, holy, holy, Lord God Almighty, which was, and is, and is to come. And when those beasts give glory and honour and thanks to him that sat on the throne, who liveth for ever and ever, The four and twenty elders fall down before him that sat on the throne, and worship him that liveth for ever and ever, and cast their crowns before

the throne, saying, Thou art worthy, O Lord, to receive glory and honour and power: for thou hast created all things, and for thy pleasure they are and were created. (Revelation 4:1, 2, 8-11)

Praise, for a new believer, can look very strange. Praise is loud, and it calls for involvement. People want you to sing, clap and lift your hands, jump for joy, and bow to the King. There are biblical basics for everything a praiser does.

Key #1 Hallelujah

Hallelujah is the chief word in the Bible that was translated as "praise." It is the only word that is the same in all languages. The word, hallelujah, is known as the linguistic test of all Christian worshipers no matter what country they come from or language they speak. The word hallelujah occurs 160 times in the Old Testament. "Halal" means to boast, to make a show, to rave about, to celebrate, and "jah" means Jehovah (God). Therefore, hallelujah means to boast on or to show off God (Meeks, 1996). Stated below are three examples of the word hallelujah that were translated as "praise."

Seven times a day do I praise thee because of thy righteous judgments. (Psalm 119:164)

Praise ye the LORD. Praise, O ye servants of the LORD, praise the name of the LORD. Blessed be the name of the LORD from this time forth and for evermore. From the rising of the sun unto the going down of the same the LORD's name is to be praised. (Psalm 113:1-3)

And he appointed certain of the Levites to minister before the ark of the LORD, and to record, and to thank and praise the LORD God of Israel... Give thanks unto the LORD, call upon his name, make known his deeds among the people. Sing unto him, sing psalms unto him, talk ye of all his wondrous works. Glory ye in his holy name: let the heart of them rejoice that seek the LORD. (1 Chronicles 16: 4, 8-10)

Key #2 Yadah

The Hebrew word "Yadah" was translated as "praise" fifty-two times in the Old Testament. Yadah means "to hold out your hands, to admire, look up to, or worship with extended hands." Yadah is expressing to God that everything I have, I gladly give up to your authority; I will not resist you in any way; I am willingly submitting to you. Yadah also means to surrender or to relinquish (to give up) possession or control to God willingly. Lifting up your hands is a universal sign of surrender (Meeks, 1996). During that time of lifting hands, it allows God to look at one's heart in order to see the purpose of the person's action, to deal with one's problems or sins. Here are scriptures with Yadah translated as "praise."

Thus will I bless thee while I live: I will lift up my hands in thy name. (Psalm 63:4)

I will bless the LORD at all times: his praise *shall* continually *be* in my mouth. My soul shall make her boast in the LORD: the humble shall hear *thereof*, and be glad. O magnify the LORD with me, and let us exalt his name together. (Psalm 34:1-3)

I will therefore that men pray every where, lifting up holy hands, without wrath and doubting. (1 Timothy 2:8)

Leah's story

Leah was Laban's daughter, the first wife of Jacob, and the older sister of Rachel. Laban, Jacob's uncle, deceived him by giving him Leah instead of Rachel on the wedding night(Genesis 29:21-25). Leah was forced into a marriage with a man who did not love her. However, she always showed love and loyalty toward her husband. Leah was raised in a home that worshipped idol gods. These idols were small figurines of female deities; they were supposed to promise fertility, and whoever possessed them upon the owner's death had a right to his estate when he died. Rachel, Jacob's second wife, depended on those gods for religious and divination purposes: protection, inheritance rights, and fertility. When Jacob departed from his uncle's house, Rachel stole her father's gods (Genesis 31:19).

God had decided to open Leah's womb to have children when He saw that Jacob did not love her (Genesis 29:31). In each pregnancy, Leah realized that God had intervened on her behalf. After Leah gave birth to three sons, she hoped that a connection or bond would develop between her and Jacob. However, when the fourth son was born, Leah's focus changed from man (her husband Jacob) to God.

> And Leah conceived, and bare a son, and she called his name Reuben: for she said, Surely the LORD hath looked upon my affliction; now therefore my husband will love me. And she conceived again, and bare a son; and said, Because the LORD hath heard that I *was* hated, he hath therefore given me this *son* also: and she called his name Simeon. And she conceived again, and bare a son; and said, Now this time will my husband be joined unto me, because I have born him three sons: therefore was his name called Levi. And she conceived again, and bare a son: and she said, Now will I praise [Yadah] the LORD: therefore she called his name Judah; and left bearing. (Genesis 29:32-35)

Now that this time has passed, let us document the blessings that God granted Leah and her children. First, one-half of all the tribes of Israel (Jacob) were born from Leah's womb (Genesis 35:23). Second, the priesthood of Israel comes from the tribe of Levi. Jacob warned all of his children of Simeon and Levi's anger. They took pleasure in killing. Those two tribes, Simeon and Levi, should be scatted among the other tribes of Israel (Genesis 49:5-7). However, God had good use for the tribe of Levi in the priesthood. When Moses was gone for a long period of time, the children of Israel started to serve other gods. They even molded a golden calf with the help of Aaron, the future first High Priest. However, when Moses returned and saw how corrupt they had become, he was angry. "Then Moses stood in the gate of the camp, and said, Who *is* on the LORD'S side? *let him come* unto me. And all the sons of Levi gathered themselves together unto him." The Levites committed a great massacre that day. Three thousands Israelites were murdered by their hands. They killed their neighbors, friends, and brothers (Exodus 32:26-29). Jacob had warned them of Simon and Levi's nature. After that event, only the tribe of Levi was allowed to do the service of the temple. Moses and Aaron were from the tribe of Levi. Moses was a great leader who brought the Israelites out of the land of Egypt. He authored the Pentateuch. Aaron was Moses'spokesperson and the first High Priest in Israel. Third, all the Kings of Judah and some of the kings of Israel come from the tribe of Judah (Genesis 49:8-12). Some of these Kings are listed in Jesus' genealogy (Matthew 1:1-16).

King David—He was the greatest King of Israel. He was a skillful musician. David unified Israel through military and economic expansion. He made sure that Jerusalem would become Israel's religious center (2 Samuel 6; 1 Chronicles 13, 15, 16). King David was humble enough to glorify God (2 Samuel 22). His life teaches us that God's forgiveness does not remove the consequence of sin.

King Solomon—He was the third King of Israel. King Solomon built God's Temple in Jerusalem. He was the wisest man who ever lived. The Lord appeared to Solomon in a dream and asked him what his fondest desire was. Solomon asked for wisdom to judge Israel, and God was pleased (1 Kings 3). His wish, along with the gift of long life, riches, and fame, was granted.

King Jehoshaphat—The fourth King of Judah. His successful rule was due to his religious policy. Everyone in Judah brought tribute to King Jehoshaphat so that he had great riches and honor (2 Chronicles 17:1-5). The surrounding nations, observing the strength of Jehoshaphat and recognizing the presence of the Lord with him, not only refrained from attacking Judah but even brought tribute to him (vv. 7-11). King Jehoshaphat appointed Levites, priests, and family heads to handle cases pertaining to the worship of the Lord and to make decisions in disputes arising between citizens (2 Chronicles 19:4-11).

King Hezekiah—King of Judah. In his first month of reign, King Hezekiah opened the Temple doors and repaired them. He brought the Levites together and ordered them to sanctify themselves and the Temple and to reinstate the religious ceremonies that had long been neglected (2 Chronicles 29). When King Hezekiah became seriously ill, Isaiah, the prophet, told him to prepare for death. The king earnestly prayed for an extension of life, and God promised him 15 more years as well as deliverance from Assyrians (2 Kings 20:1-11).

King Uzziah—He came to the throne of Judah at the age of sixteen. His name means, "My strength is the Lord." King Uzziah is portrayed as one who "did what was right in the eyes of the Lord" (2 King 15:3; 2 Chronicles 26:4). The Lord blessed him in his entire mission, so that he prospered.

Fourth, Jesus' roots extend back to Leah. Jesus, the son of God, has become both the High Priest and King with the establishment of the New Covenant. The new covenant allows all nations and people to enter into an agreement with God.

Key # 3 Barak

Barak means "to kneel, in adoration to bless God." When worship happens one is willing to bow down. Bowing down is the physical activity that anyone can display, but God is looking at the attitude of humbleness of the heart. Barak is the attitude of a person, "a frame of mind affecting one thoughts or behavior" towards God. The spiritual posture, of bowing down of the heart, is saying that I am not worthy to be in God's presence, and I am willing submitting to You. Submitting to God allows him to rule your life in every area. Bowing down is a sign of saying, God, I do not deserve to be in your presence; thank you for the privilege. Now, here is man-made of the "dust of the ground" with the sentence of death upon him before he was conceived in his mother's womb. The loving God is allowing him an appearance, unthinkable. Here are few scriptures that mean Barak.

> O come, let us worship and bow down: let us kneel before the LORD our maker. (Psalm 95:6)

> Humble yourselves in the sight of the Lord, and he shall lift you up.
> (James 4:10)

> Humble yourselves therefore under the mighty hand of God, that he may exalt you in due time. (1 Peter 5:6)

Key #4 Tehillah

Tehillah "is a derivative of Hala, the emphasis of the word Tehillah is on singing of praise." It is used fifty-five times in the Old Testament. God is pleased in music. Tehillah means to sing Hallelujah (Meeks, 1995). Tehillah also means to sing forth a song of praise to God, to celebrate. In these songs, we are to boast about Him in words and music. Children of God are commanded to sing over three hundred times in the Bible. During this spiritual warfare, as the Children of God continue to praise Him, He will take inventory of our enemies. Some of our enemies are pride, depression, lust, selfishness, lack of forgiveness, poverty-stricken, sickness, etc. However, God loves music (Tehillah) so much, that he deals with one's enemies to keep the song going. He actually takes the psalmist's place in the battle. Here is a great story in the Bible that will illustrate God's mighty hand while His children demonstrate praise in many forms. This true story shows the power of faith, obedience, and Tehillah in action. When God takes on the enemy, the job is complete. No traces or roots are left to grow.

> And all Judah stood before the LORD, with their little ones, their wives, and their children. Then upon Jahaziel the son of Zechariah, the son of Benaiah, the son of Jeiel, the son of Mattaniah, a Levite of the sons of Asaph, came the Spirit of the LORD in the midst of the congregation; And he said, Hearken ye, all Judah, and ye inhabitants of Jerusalem, and thou king Jehoshaphat, Thus saith the LORD unto you, Be not afraid nor dismayed by reason of this great multitude; for the battle *is* not yours, but God's.

> To morrow go ye down against them: behold, they come up by the cliff of Ziz; and ye shall find them at the end of

the brook, before the wilderness of Jeruel. Ye shall not *need* to fight in this *battle*: set yourselves, stand ye *still*, and see the salvation of the LORD with you, O Judah and Jerusalem: fear not, nor be dismayed; to morrow go out against them: for the LORD *will be* with you.

And Jehoshaphat bowed [Barak] his head with *his* face to the ground: and all Judah and the inhabitants of Jerusalem fell [Barak] before the LORD, worshipping the LORD. And the Levites, of the children of the Kohathites, and of the children of the Korhites, stood up to praise [Tehillah] the LORD God of Israel with a loud voice [Shabach] on high.

And they rose early in the morning, and went forth into the wilderness of Tekoa: and as they went forth, Jehoshaphat stood and said, Hear me, O Judah, and ye inhabitants of Jerusalem; Believe in the LORD your God, so shall ye be established; believe his prophets, so shall ye prosper. [Hallelujah] And when he had consulted with the people, he appointed singers [Tehillah] unto the LORD, and that should praise the beauty of holiness, as they went out before the army, and to say,

Praise [Hallelujah] the LORD; for his mercy *endureth* for ever. **And when they began to sing** [Tehillah] **and to praise,** [Hallelujah] the LORD set ambushments against the children of Ammon, Moab, and mount Seir, which were come against Judah; and they were smitten. For the children of Ammon and Moab stood up against the inhabitants of mount Seir, utterly to slay and destroy *them*: and when they had made an end of the inhabitants of Seir, every one helped to destroy another. And when Judah came toward the watch tower in the wilderness, they looked unto the multitude, and, behold, they *were* dead bodies fallen to the earth, and none escaped. (2 Chronicles 20:13-24)

Key # 5 Zamar

Zamar means "to play music, to touch the strings or parts of a musical instrument, to make music, accompanied by the voice." The Bible goes into details of the different instruments used during praise. Do not feel restricted in choosing an instrument to play.

> Praise him with the sound of the trumpet: praise him with the psaltery and harp. Praise him with the timbrel and dance: praise him with stringed instruments and organs. Praise him upon the loud cymbals: praise him upon the high sounding cymbals. (Psalm 150:3-5)

Singing praise to God is wonderful, but the addition of musical instruments helps to express the inner feelings of the worshiper. Music sometimes helps the worshiper to focus on their thoughts of God's goodness. It helps to tune out the people standing or sitting around them. Music helps the physical acts of praise to be elevated to the spiritual realm. In the Old Testament, the Levites and priest praised the LORD day by day, singing to the LORD, accompanied by loud instruments (2 Chronicles 30:21). The priests and King David understand the significance of music in the praising experience. King David got into the Zamar part of the praise experience, too. He had four thousand Levites play instruments during one praise and worship service. Imagine the sound and power that was released at that time and place.

> Moreover four thousand *were* porters; and four thousand praised the LORD with the instruments which I made, *said David*, to praise *therewith*. (1 Chronicles 23:5 NKJV)

Music can be used for the glory of God. It helps create an atmosphere for the spiritual gifts to operate. For example, the prophet Elisha used music when he prophesized to God's people.

> And Jehoshaphat said, The word of the LORD is with him. So the king of Israel and Jehoshaphat and the king of Edom went down to him. And Elisha said unto the king of Israel, What have I to do with thee? get thee to the prophets of thy father, and to the prophets of thy mother. And the king of Israel said unto him, Nay: for the LORD hath called these three kings together, to deliver them into the hand of Moab. And Elisha said, As the LORD of hosts liveth, before whom I stand, surely, were it not that I regard the presence of Jehoshaphat the king of Judah, I would not look toward thee, nor see thee. But now bring me a minstrel. And it came to pass, when the minstrel played, that the hand of the LORD came upon him. (2 King 3:12-15)

Key #6 Towdah

Towdah means "to express thanks." It is to show extensions of hands in a sacrifice and to lift oneself up to God (Meeks, 1996). A **sacrifice of praise** is to offer what you do not possess. To offer praise to God even when you do not feel like it. Towdah is to thank God for something to happen, which has not manifested yet. One should shout just like it already has happened. This is a form of displaying one's faith. Bless God before you receive the blessing that falls within his will. Let us look at Hannah's story. It is a perfect example of Towdah. Hannah has offered up to God her son, but she was barren. She had no son.

> And she was in bitterness of soul, and prayed unto the LORD, and wept sore. And she vowed a vow, and said, O LORD of hosts, if thou wilt indeed look on the affliction of

thine handmaid, and remember me, and not forget thine handmaid, but wilt give unto thine handmaid a man child, then I will give him unto the LORD all the days of his life, and there shall no razor come upon his head. And it came to pass, as she continued praying before the LORD, that Eli marked her mouth. Now Hannah, she spake in her heart; only her lips moved, but her voice was not heard: therefore Eli thought she had been drunken. And Eli said unto her, How long wilt thou be drunken? put away thy wine from thee. And Hannah answered and said, No, my lord, I *am* a woman of a sorrowful spirit: I have drunk neither wine nor strong drink, but have poured out my soul before the LORD. Count not thine handmaid for a daughter of Belial: for out of the abundance of my complaint and grief have I spoken hitherto. Then Eli answered and said, Go in peace: and the God of Israel grant *thee* thy petition that thou hast asked of him. And she said, Let thine handmaid find grace in thy sight. So the woman went her way, and did eat, and her countenance was no more *sad*. And they rose up in the morning early, and worshipped before the LORD, and returned, and came to their house to Ramah: and Elkanah knew Hannah his wife; and the LORD remembered her. Wherefore it came to pass, when the time was come about after Hannah had conceived, that she bare a son, and called his name Samuel, *saying*, Because I have asked him of the LORD. (1 Samuel 1:10-20)

Hannah kept her word and gave Samuel to the priest, Eli, to be use by God. Hannah later had three more sons and two daughters (1 Samuel 1:28; 2:21).

In this spiritual war, the writer Habakkuk uses the terms **deer feet**. When a hunter is tracking a deer, the deer seem to move more quickly and lightly. To make a run lighter, sometimes one will have to remove some things or someone from your life. In the midst of losing physical things that are temporary in nature, the worshiper is gaining spiritual things for life everlasting. Events that happen in people's lives help to push them into their destiny or purpose in God. The idea's place to run is to a stream. Water is used to wash, to help clean things. Some places in God's people are not ready yet because they are too spiritually dirty. Therefore they need to be washed by the Word of God (Ephesians 5:25, 26). It has been said that the hunter's dogs lose the sense of the deer as they pass through water. The children of God have enemies in heavenly places. When Christians sin, or fail to respond to their obligations, or are ready to go higher in God, the enemies are quick to report their transgression to God. As one makes swift to the praise of God, the enemies are still following. The Word of God is a Christian sword in of the spiritual realm. The writer refers to the next step by using three major words, **"go on"** and **"heights."** To **"go on"** means that the run is not over. Continue on your Christian journey, death is not at your door. In addition, the word **"heights"** means spiritual growth and maturity has occurred.

> Although the fig tree shall not blossom, neither *shall* fruit *be* in the vines; the labour of the olive shall fail, and the fields shall yield no meat; the flock shall be cut off from the fold, and *there shall be* no herd in the stalls: Yet I will rejoice in the LORD, I will joy in the God of my salvation. The LORD God *is* my strength, and he will make my feet like hinds' *feet*, and he will make me to walk upon mine high places. To the chief singer on my stringed instruments. (Habakkuk 3:17-19)

This is the time when one is tired, exhausted, worn-out, drained, hurt, has low self-esteem, no sense of worth, no confidence in yourself, the children are acting up, and the bills are due, but the money is short. Still praise God with thanksgiving in your heart. Towdah is always having an attitude of thanks no matter what the situation, and move on.

Key # 7 Shabach

"Shabach" means "to address in a loud tone, to shout to God in a loud tone, to command glory, triumph." There are times people should not be quiet. God has been so good, and they are not embarrassed who knows about their joy. Being loud means that a person is excited, and they are willing to share their experience with whoever wants to know. Joy and happiness overtake a person's normal mannerisms; an inner explosion happens. A person's innermost part of thanksgiving has overflowed that they cannot hold their expression. Then one displays uncontrollable praise, dancing, crying, the clapping of hands, etc. People today play their music so loud in their cars that when they pass your house the windows shake. That is similar to Shabach. There is a wonderful example of how loud and excited praise should be.

> In the year that king Uzziah died I saw also the Lord sitting upon a throne, high and lifted up, and his train filled the temple. Above it stood the seraphims: each one had six wings; with twain he covered his face, and with twain he covered his feet, and with twain he did fly. And one cried unto another, and said, Holy, holy, holy, *is* the LORD of hosts: the whole earth *is* full of his glory. And the posts of the door moved at the voice of him that cried, and the house was filled with smoke.
> (Isaiah 6:1-4)

The posts were hopping around, moving during the praise service because of the loud tone of excitement that the worshiper was displaying toward God.

In summary, the seven different Hebrew words: Hallelujah, Yadah, Barak, Tehillah, Zamar, Towdah, and Shabach in the Old Testament were translated "praise." The biblical explanation in details shows us how praise works along with their biblical scriptures to clarify how the Hebrew words of praise can be used in life. Praise does not happen by accident, but on purpose. Each act of praise is very deep and significant for a Christian's survival.

Chapter Three

The World's Greatest Asset

Chapter three will explain the position of humanity in the universe today. Why did God create man? What rights and liberties does man possess? What is man's potential destiny? The most valuable asset God has created on earth is man. An asset is "an item of value owned." Man was created in God's image and His likeness. An image is "a visual representation of something." It is as if God is looking in a mirror and the representation reflected back is man. Man has not operated in his full authority, because the enemies have attacked man's greatest power and resource: his confidence, and self-esteem. Lack of self-esteem has crippled humanity and caused a lack in individual lives. Why does humanity have such powerful enemies? These enemies will be explained in chapter four.

God has made man for a reason. God was looking for someone to have fellowship with, so He made man in His image. When man was created, he was made complete. God has given man dominion (rule), crowned with authority over all the earth and creatures. Here comes a mystery. Humanity now has the potential to be like Jesus, adopted sons and daughters of God. This is why Satan and his evil host are enemies of humanity. Man has the right to mold and direct his future with his own words. "Death and life *are* in the power of the tongue: and they that love it shall eat the fruit thereof" (Proverbs 18:21).

> Now I say, *That* the heir, as long as he is a child, differeth nothing from a servant, though he be lord of all; But is under tutors and governors until the time appointed of the

father. Even so we, when we were children, were in bond-age under the elements of the world: But when the fulness of the time was come, God sent forth his Son, made of a woman, made under the law, To redeem them that were under the law, that we might receive the adoption of sons. (Galatians 4:1-5)

Blessed *be* the God and Father of our Lord Jesus Christ, who hath blessed us with all spiritual blessings in heav-enly *places* in Christ: According as he hath chosen us in him before the foundation of the world, that we should be holy and without blame before him in love: Having predes-tinated us unto the adoption of children by Jesus Christ to himself, according to the good pleasure of his will, To the praise of the glory of his grace, wherein he hath made us accepted in the beloved. (Ephesians 1:3-6)

Apostles in the Making

Christians sometimes have a lack of self-esteem, "a confidence and sat-isfaction in oneself." Self-esteem is like salt. If salt has lost it saltiness, it cannot be called salt. After faith, self-esteem is the inner man action or powerhouse. The devil does not want God's people to know their value and potential. If the devil can make one doubt their own self-worth, he knows that a defective individual is no good for him/herself or for God. You can forget your Spiritual gift or growth. A Christian's lacks of self-esteem sometimes come from one's past sinful life. It causes one to carry around a cloud of condemnation, to be pronouncing guilt, unfit for use. We think that we do not deserve forgiveness no matter now much we pray, fast, and praise God. The devil has deceit us. The Bible shows the account of the weakness of two powerful men. God used them very ef-fectively for the building of His Kingdom (Meeks, 1996). God has a use for us, too.

Peter was one of the twelve disciples, and later became an Apostle that followed Jesus while he was here on earth. Peter was a fisherman, married with children. He walked along with Jesus during his ministry (Matthew 4:18-20). Peter was one of the inner three that followed Jesus whenever only a few people were allowed to escort him. He saw and heard the teachings of Jesus. He witnessed Jesus performing miracles, healing, and casting out demons from possessed people (Matthew 4:23, 24). All of Jesus' disciples, along with Peter, witnessed Jesus when he raised Lazarus from the dead (John 11:14-16, 38-44). There came a time when Jesus asked his disciples who they thought he was; the Holy Spirit imparted the answer to Peter of Jesus' proper identity (Matthew 16:13-17). Peter was the first of Jesus' disciples to whom God started to reveal spiritual things. He had childlike behavior when it came to seeking wisdom and understanding of God's word. When Jesus was teaching about forgiveness, it was Peter who asked the Lord to explain forgiveness to him (Matthew 18:21).

Peter also had some issues in his life that need to be studied. Peter was impulsive, rash, and he often was the first to speak his mind. His character had three weaknesses that were opposed to his potential goals of godly behavior. First, Peter displayed courage, but at the same time, he committed a criminal offense of violence and impulsiveness against the high priest's servant. He was trying to resist Jesus' arrest. He pulled out a sword and cut off a man's ear. Peter showed a lot of courage in defending Jesus in that way. Peter was ready to fight in an instant.

> Then Simon Peter having a sword drew it, and smote the high priest's servant, and cut off his right ear. The servant's name was Malchus. (John 18:10)

Second, Peter had an inconsistency with his faith. He was the first disciple to demonstrate his faith, but at the same time doubt had set in. Jesus told his disciples to get in a boat and go to the other side, and he was going to meet them there later. While the disciples were in the boat at night, they spotted Jesus walking on the water toward them. By faith, Peter called out to Jesus asking permission to join him. Peter got out of the boat during a storm and walked on the water toward Jesus. He demonstrated both courage and faith.

> And when the disciples saw him walking on the sea, they were troubled, saying, It is a spirit; and they cried out for fear. But straightway Jesus spake unto them, saying, Be of good cheer; it is I; be not afraid. And Peter answered him and said, Lord, if it be thou, bid me come unto thee on the water. And he said, Come. And when Peter was come down out of the ship, he walked on the water, to go to Jesus. But when he saw the wind boisterous, he was afraid; and beginning to sink, he cried, saying, Lord, save me. And immediately Jesus stretched forth *his* and, and caught him, and said unto him, O thou of little faith, wherefore didst thou doubt? (Matthew 14:26-31)

Third, Peter had expressed his loyalty and commitment to Jesus, but also he displayed denying, lying, and swearing. Before Jesus' trial, he warned Peter about his destiny that would soon occur. Peter did not take to heart what Jesus was saying because he knew that his loyalty and commitment lay with Jesus. He told Peter that Peter would turn away from him, but a plan of escape was set in motion for him. Peter was instructed to strengthen his brothers after he went through his ordeal.

> And the Lord said, Simon, Simon, behold, Satan hath desired *to have* you, that he may sift *you* as wheat: But I have prayed for thee, that thy faith fail not: and when thou art converted, strengthen thy brethren. And he said unto him, Lord, I am ready to go with thee, both into prison, and to death. And he said, I tell thee, Peter, the cock shall not

crow this day, before that thou shalt thrice deny that thou knowest me. (Luke 22:31-34)

Peter did precisely what Jesus said. During Jesus' trial, Peter denied and lied about his relationship with Jesus to the point that he was swearing at people. When he realized what he had done, he cried to the point that he thought God had no use for him.

And after a while came unto *him* they that stood by, and said to Peter, Surely thou also art *one* of them; for thy speech bewrayeth thee. Then began he to curse and to swear, *saying*, I know not the man. And immediately the cock crew. And Peter remembered the word of Jesus, which said unto him, Before the cock crow, thou shalt deny me thrice. And he went out, and wept bitterly. (Matthew 26:73-75)

Now that all of these events had happened in Peter's life, God still had use for him. After the crucifixion, two women went to anoint Jesus' body, but they did not find it. An angel told them to give a message to Jesus' disciples and Peter (Mark 16:7). Peter's name was the only one singled out by the angel. It was an indication that God still had purpose for his life. Peter preached the first sermon in the Book of Acts (Chapter Two) on the Day of Pentecost. He told the people to repent and be baptized for the remission of sins (Acts 2:38, 41). As a result, about three thousand people received salvation that day. Peter wrote two books in the New Testament: First and Second Peter. The same mouth that denied Jesus, cursed and swore, was still of use to God.

Whenever you mess up, do not think God is through with you. God still loves you. Dry your tears, dust yourselves off, hold your head up high, and bless the Lord who made heaven and earth (Meeks, 1996). If you have breath in your body, it is not over. In Proverbs 24:16, it declares that

"For a just *man* falleth seven times, and riseth up again..." So, rise, my brother, rise, my sister, and let the power of God use you for His purpose.

The second apostle who had some major issues in his life is Paul. Paul was a Pharisee from the tribe of Benjamin (Philippians 3:5 NLT). Paul's name was Saul, just like the first king of Israel: he was also a Benjaminite. Unlike Peter, Paul was very educated. He studied under Gamaliel the books of the Law and Prophets and the Hebrew and Aramaic languages (Acts 21:40). His father taught him the trade of the tent maker. Paul was single. His Christian journey started after Jesus had already ascended to heaven.

Paul oppressed the church by breathed threats (talking strong about) and murder against the disciples of the Lord. He went to the high priest in Jerusalem to obtain a letter to authorize him to arrest the believers and to bring them to Jerusalem for trail (Acts 9:1, 2). Paul was no respecter of gender; he took both men and women, going from house to house looking for Christians. Stephen was the first Christian to be martyred. Paul stood by, approved, and witnessed his death (Acts 6:9-15; 7:51-60).

Later, after having a confrontation with Jesus, this same man Paul became a very powerful man for Christ, so much so that the Jews turned on him and plotted to kill him. The Lord told Ananias, one of his servants, to anointed Paul eyes to receive his sight because God has need for him, "But the Lord said unto him, Go thy way: for he [Paul] is a chosen vessel unto me, to bear my name before the Gentiles, and kings, and the children of Israel" (Acts 9:10-15). Every thing Paul did, he did with all of his might. After his conversion, he immediately started preaching "Christ in the synagogues, that he is the Son of God" (Acts 9:19-23).

Paul wrote thirteen books in the New Testament. He was the apostle to the Gentiles. His main message was that forgiveness and eternal life are available to all people.

Now, let us talk about us. God knows our sins. Our past is no secret to Him. God knows we were going to sin, "For all have sinned, and come short of the glory of God" (Romans 3:23). However, God had a plan for our lives before the world came into existence.

> According as he hath chosen us in him before the foun-
> dation of the world, that we should be holy and without
> blame before him in love: Having predestinated us unto
> the adoption of children by Jesus Christ to himself, ac-
> cording to the good pleasure of his will. (Ephesians 1:4, 5)

God loves us. The Bible tells us that "charity [love] shall cover the multitude of sins" (1 Peter 4:8). However, that does not give us permission to purposely sin. God loves sinners, not the sin. Salvation is the plan that separates the sins from the sinner.

> But God commendeth his love toward us, in that, while
> we were yet sinners, Christ died for us…..For if, when we
> were enemies, we were reconciled to God by the death of
> his Son, much more, being reconciled, we shall be saved
> by his life. (Romans 5:8, 10)

The Value of Man

Now, what makes us valuable? Six things establish value. Number one, **the qualification of the maker** of an object gives value/worth. A watch made by Timex is not as valuable as a Rolex; however, they both will give you the correct time. A Chevy car is not as valuable as a Mercedes, yet they both can transport you from one place to another. There can be two identical houses built side by side. Scott Peterson, who nobody knows, built the first house, and Frank Lloyd Wright built the other house. They can sell the first house for two hundred thousand dollars while selling the other house for one million dollars. The reputation of the maker of the sec-ond house adds value to the house. Now, take a thirty-second look in the mirror at God's creation. The same God who made heaven and earth, and the God that has mercy on all generations. God made the watchmaker, carmakers, famous painters, and the house builder. You know they make purses and belts that people love to leave the tags on, because people are trying to make an impression that they have possession of a very valuable item, they have the top of the line product. Now, Christians having a very good maker, we need to start wearing our tag. Our tag would say, "These things I command you, that ye love one another" (John 15:17). We are God's creation. Not only did God make us because he wanted to, but God saved us before he made us (Meeks, 1996).

Second, we are valuable because we are **rare.** Whenever the demand for an object is great, but the number of the objects is less, the object goes up in value. Now let's glance at us. Jesus was talking to his disciples and said, "The harvest truly *is* plenteous, but the labourers *are* few" (Matthew 9:37). We are in great demand. I will take this thought further. Look around, whom do you not see? The answer is you. There is nobody like you in this universe. You are 1/1, one of a kind. You are an original and that carries great value (Meeks, 1996).

Third, they call a thing that gives value to an object **personal preference.** God has chosen to make us. We are God's choice (Meeks, 1996). Not only has God made us, but He makes us over again when we mess up (Jeremiah 18:4-11).

> And God said, Let us make man in our image, after our likeness... And the LORD God formed man of the dust of the ground, and breathed into his nostrils the breath of life; and man became a living soul. (Genesis 1:26; 2:7)

> And the vessel that he made of clay was marred [messed up] in the hand of the potter: so he made it again another vessel, as seemed good to the potter to make *it*. (Jeremiah 18:4)

This is how we (the vessels) come to Christ (messed up), sinners and on our way to hell. When we give ourselves to Christ, we actually put our life into his hands and allow God to have His way. Therefore, God makes and mold us unto what he wants us to be, that is what is **good** to Him (the potter). A potter shapes and molds the clay as he turns it on his table. Second, he puts the vessel into a fire in order for it to keep its shape, to burn out all impurities to let the luster and shine to set in. Later he runs the vessel under water to wash away the residue.

> O house of Israel, cannot I do with you as this potter? saith the LORD. Behold, as the clay *is* in the potter's hand, so *are* ye in mine hand, O house of Israel. (Jeremiah 18:6)

God has a purpose for us. He has defined goals and jobs in his kingdom just for each of us. "For I know the thoughts that I think toward you [put your name right there], saith the LORD, thoughts of peace, and not of evil, to give you an expected end" (Jeremiah 29:11).

The fourth thing that gives value is **potential worth**. Potential means hidden but not yet developed (Meeks, 1996). Here are a few things that have potential worth: saving bonds, old coins, stamp collection, stocks, mutual funds, and land (property). We purchase these items for one amount, but sell or cash them in for more money than when we purchase them. For example, you can buy a house for fifty thousand dollars and fifteen years later sell the house for eighty-five thousand dollars. We have a great potential worth. In every Christian, there is the potential to be like Jesus.

> Beloved, now are we the sons of God, and it doth not yet appear what we shall be: but we know that, when he shall appear, we shall be like him; for we shall see him as he is. (1 John 3:2)

The fifth thing that gives value is **permanence.** People say things that last a long time have great value, for instance a Kirby vacuum cleaner. That is why people do not mind paying more money for it, because it lasts a long time. Another one is a Mercedes Benz or even job security, because how long an object lasts or how long you have a job is what makes it of great value (Meeks, 1996). Now, we will see how long we will last.

> For we know that if our earthly house [our physical bodies] of *this* tabernacle were dissolved [destroyed], we have a building of God, an house not made with hands, eternal in the heavens.... We are confident, *I say*, and willing rather to be absent from the body, and to be present with the Lord. (2 Corinthians 5:1, 8)

See, that is why Jesus, our older brother, told us he will get things ready for our homecoming in John 14:2, 3.

The last thing that gives value to an object is the **price tag**, what it costs. That is why we are all telling people what we paid for things. We know that a gold chain for ten dollars is not real. The last thing that determines our value is the price tag, what God has paid for us (Meeks, 1996). John 3:16 says, "For God so loved the world, that he gave his only begotten Son, that whosoever believeth in him should not perish, but have everlasting life." We cost God his only begotten Son. We cost more than the stars, moon, oceans, sun, kings, queens, or the governor. God turned around, looked at his Son, and said, nothing is more valuable in the universe than you (Jesus). God has put all things under his (Jesus') feet. God said, I have some people on their way to Hell. Come here, my Son; I will pay my Son, for my people. Jesus said, I love them so much, so I will pay for them with my own blood (Meeks, 1996).

> What? know ye not that your body is the temple of the Holy Ghost *which is* in you, which ye have of God, and ye are not your own? For ye [Put your name right there] are **bought with a price**: therefore glorify God in your body, and in your spirit, which are God's. (1 Corinthians 6:19, 20)

> Take heed therefore unto yourselves, and to all the flock, over the which the Holy Ghost hath made you overseers,

to feed the church of God, which **he** [JESUS] **hath pur-
chased with his own blood**. (Acts 20:28)

We praise God because we are valuable. Humanity (people) is the
world's greatest asset. We are the most valuable thing God has created.
We have a good maker (God), we are scarce (one of a kind), we are God's
personal preference, His choice (he made us because he wanted to), we
have a good potential worth (we have the potential to like Christ), and we
are permanent (we will be with God always). We carry the highest price in
the universe. Our price tag says **the blood of Christ**. That is enough to
bow down and worship God forever! Hallelujah! (Meeks, 1996).

Chapter Four

Benefits of Praise

Praise and worship are not just physical activities to make one feel good. The spiritual attributes helps humanity to be all it can be now and after the second coming of Christ. What is man's potential? The human race has three great potentials: first, to become the sons and daughters of God; second, to avoid the second death; and third, to rule with Jesus Christ for a thousand years (Revelation 20:6). Have you heard the saying, "When praises go up, blessings come down?" These blessings help humanity to reach its potential because these blessings create freedom. However, only three blessings will be covered in this book. The first blessing is that praise makes the enemy shut up. Making the enemies shut up allows the praiser to hear the Word of God; therefore, faith can develop. The second blessing is that praise neutralizes depression. Depression is usually the results of believing the lies of the enemies, Satan and the demonic host. Neutralizing the lies of the Devil create hope. The participant is in the position of believing the report of the Lord. The third blessing of praise is deliverance. Christians will have the freedom to move forward in their destiny, to flow in their Spiritual gifts. They will be able to grow, develop, and mature as children of God—therefore, to be transformed into the image of Christ.

History of Satan and His Host

Believe it or not, some struggles are good for Christians. If they are going to overcome, they need to understand this struggle, this fight, this

Spiritual war that is going on, and learn how to avoid being captured by the enemies. The enemy wants to kill and totally bind Christians: physically, mentally, and spiritually (John 10:10). Nevertheless, God has given humanity praise to use as a weapon so they can help themselves to stay alive and free. We have to realize that we will not win all of the battles against the evil forces against us. However, we will win the war. God has warned us of this fact, that Satan has a well-organized evil army. Knowing the enemy can help ease the path on this journey. Listed below are two scriptures that gives insight of this Spiritual battle. First is the organization of the enemy, second how Christians are to react during the battle.

> Put on the whole armour of God, that ye may be able to stand against the wiles of the devil. For we wrestle not against flesh and blood, but against principalities, against powers, against the rulers of the darkness of this world, against spiritual wickedness in high *places*. (Ephesians 6:11, 12)

> I know thy works, and tribulation, and poverty, (but thou art rich) and *I know* the blasphemy of them which say they are Jews, and are not, but *are* the synagogue of Satan. Fear none of those things which thou shalt suffer: behold, the devil shall cast *some* of you into prison, that ye may be tried; and ye shall have tribulation ten days: be thou faithful unto death, and I will give thee a crown of life. He that hath an ear, let him hear what the Spirit saith unto the churches; He that overcometh shall not be hurt of the second death. (Revelation 2:9-11)

Why does this spiritual war exist? How did it get started? What active role does humanity have in the war? The answers to these questions will help clarify why life can be so hard. Satan's beginning was one of beauty, holiness, and atonement to God. His name was Lucifer. He was an anointed guardian cherub of God, created blameless without spot, wrinkle, or blemish. His first job was a praise and worship leader in heaven. However, as time went on, he has decided for himself that he wanted to be praised; he wanted to be like God. This is what caused the connection between God and Lucifer to be broken. The bond was so broken that his name was changed to Satan. The word Satan means, "the chief of evil spirits, the great adversary of humanity." Now, Satan has received his sentence from God. However, it has not happened yet. Right now, he is the prince of the power of the air, making trouble for all those who still think God name is worthy to be praised. Let us take a look in the book of Ezekiel at Satan's beginning and his future.

Moreover the word of the LORD came unto me, saying, Son of man, take up a lamentation upon the king of Tyrus, and say unto him, Thus saith the Lord GOD; Thou sealest up the sum, full of wisdom, and perfect in beauty. Thou hast been in Eden the garden of God; every precious stone *was* thy covering, the sardius, topaz, and the diamond, the beryl, the onyx, and the jasper, the sapphire, the emerald, and the carbuncle, and gold: the workmanship of thy tabrets and of thy pipes was prepared in thee in the day that thou wast created. Thou *art* the anointed cherub that covereth; and I have set thee *so*: thou wast upon the holy mountain of God; thou hast walked up and down in the midst of the stones of fire. Thou *wast* perfect in thy ways from the day that thou wast created, till iniquity was found in thee. By the **multitude of thy merchandise** they have filled the midst of thee with violence, and thou hast sinned: therefore I will cast thee as profane out of the mountain of God: and I will destroy thee, O covering cherub, from the midst of the stones of fire. Thine heart was lifted up because of thy beauty, thou hast **corrupted thy wisdom** by reason of thy brightness: I will cast thee to the ground, I will lay thee before kings, that they may behold thee. Thou hast **defiled thy sanctuaries** by the multitude of thine iniquities, by the iniquity of thy traffic; therefore will I bring forth a fire from the midst of thee, it shall devour thee, and I will bring thee to ashes upon the earth in the sight of all them that behold thee. All they that know thee among the people shall be astonished at thee: thou shalt be a terror, and never *shalt* thou *be* any more. (Ezekiel 28:11-19)

In the above scripture, there were three phases used, that will clarify what Satan has done. The first phase is "**multitude of thy merchandise**," which means to "exchange." The second phase is "**corrupted thy wisdom**" which means found "guilty of dishonest practices" sin. The third phase is "**defiled thy sanctuaries**" which mean "to divest of sacred to a profane use or purpose, to pollute, dishonor." When Satan tried to exalt (revere) himself, he was saying, nobody wants to praise you, God. A person wants to exalt (elevate) and praise themselves; nobody wants to put you above themselves. Satan was saying, God, you made a mistake. We do not want to honor you, but we want to honor ourselves. God kicked Satan out of heaven and the fight begins. This fight is actually between God and Satan, and humanity is stuck in the middle. This is why the devil and the demonic host help man so much to choose self over God. Every time a Christian sins, that gives Satan a chance to laugh at God. Also, Satan is jealous of man. In Psalm 8:4-6 the question was asked, "What is man, that thou art mindful of him? and the son of man, that thou visitest him? or thou hast made him a little lower than the angels, and hast crowned him with glory and honour. Thou madest him to have dominion over the works of thy hands; thou hast put all *things* under his feet." Here is a story that illustrates this point. There was a man who had a good woman, but he messed it up and lost the woman. Now another man has that same woman. Every time the first man sees that woman, he has to think how good he had it. The Devil feels that way about God. Whenever the Devil hears the saints giving praise to God, it reminds him what he used to possess and what is to come.

Praise Make the Enemy Shut Up

Along with obedience, praise is the chief weapon against the Devil. Satan's goal is to have Christians bound and in bondage. God wants people to be free and loose. Praise produces freedom by making the devil to shut up. When the enemy is silenced, man can have an opportunity to listen to God. 1 Peter 5:8 describes the devil as a lion. A lion has a loud roar, trying to frighten someone and to devour an individual. Satan is making noise in every situation that arises in people lives. Both the Old and New Testaments tell about the power of praise and the effects it has on the mouth of the evil heavenly host. "Out of the mouth of babes and sucklings hast thou ordained strength because of thine enemies, that thou mightest still the enemy and the avenger" (Psalm 8:2).

> And the blind and the lame came to him in the temple; and he healed them. And when the chief priests and scribes saw the wonderful things that he did, and the children crying in the temple, and saying, Hosanna to the son of David; they were sore displeased, And said unto him, Hearest thou what these say? And Jesus saith unto them, Yea; have ye never read, Out of the mouth of babes and sucklings thou hast perfected praise? (Matthew 21:14-16)

The freedom to hear the Word of God is essential for spiritual growth and maturity. "So then faith *cometh* by hearing, and hearing by the word of God" (Romans 10:17). "But without faith *it is* impossible to please *him*: for he that cometh to God must believe that he is, and *that* he is a rewarder of them that diligently seek him" (Hebrews 11:6). This is like feeding a child. Children need proper nutrients in order to develop their bones, teeth, muscles, etc. Praising God makes the enemies shut up, in order for a person to hear God—the Word is spiritual nutrients so that proper growth can occur (if one chooses to obey). Thereby faith is produced.

From a spiritual point of view, everyone was born blind and lame. The whole world needs Jesus in order to see and walk straight. The lack of knowledge, understanding, and obedience to God's word makes one blind. Therefore, one is also lame because one is going in the wrong path. Satan, "a liar and the father of lies" (John 8:44), has blinded humanity since the Garden of Eden with his mouth (Genesis 3:4; 2 Corinthians 4:3, 4).

> Let the high praises of God be in their mouth, and a twoedged sword in their hand; To execute vengeance upon the heathen, and punishments upon the people; To bind their kings with chains, and their nobles with fetters of iron; To execute upon them the judgment written: this honour have all his saints. Praise ye the LORD. (Psalm 149:6-9)

Praise can bind all of the enemies of the saints. God has given this power to His saints to use when needed. The double-edged sword is the Word of God. The sword is used to cut things up and to kill all unrighteousness in one's life, cutting up and killing Satan's lies and schemes that are set in action. This is how this scripture works. First, one is giving praise to God. That causes the enemies to shut up and they cannot move because they are bound with fetters and shackles of iron in the spiritual realm. Then the saint can declare the Word of God (the sword), that cuts and kills the lies and schemes of the enemies. In this way, freedom to obey God and living a victorious life is possible.

Praise Neutralizes Depression

Depression is sadness, gloom, dejection (discouragement), feeling downcast, having a situation lower than the general surface, and being below the standard or norm. Depression means one has accepted a lie as being the truth. Depression is a feeling that there is no hope for your situation. Depression or heaviness is a spirit that has a goal to stop a person, then to overtake them in order to kill them. Heaviness does not come on one all at once. God's healing for depression is praise. Just like oil and water, depression and praise cannot coexist in the same heart. Praise does not mean a problem does not exist, but it says "And we know that all things work together for good to them that love God, to them who are the called according to *his* purpose" (Romans 8:28). Praise during depression demonstrates that one trusts God in the midst of the storm.

In the book of Exodus, when Moses was bringing the children of Israel out of Egypt, they fell in a deep depression. Pharaoh and his army were pursuing the Israelites with horses and chariots. The children of Israel were marching, walking in rhythm with others out of Egypt. As the army was capable of overtaking them, they preferred to be in bondage rather than have faith and depend on God. Fear was talking, and depression had set in. Just like all of humanity, the children of Israel were born into slavery, serving the taskmasters all their lives. They had no clue what freedom was or how to maintain it. At that point, the children of Israel preferred Pharaoh's rule of slavery, because they wanted to live, instead of God's way, which they did not know, freedom. In the spiritual realm, they choose Satan over God. Now that is depression. Moses started preaching faith, "And Moses said unto the people, Fear ye not, stand still, and see the salvation of the LORD, which he will show to you to day: for the Egyptians whom ye have seen to day, ye shall see them again no more for ever. The LORD shall fight for you, and ye shall hold your peace. And the LORD said unto Moses, Wherefore criest thou unto me? speak unto the children of Israel, that they go forward" (Exodus 14:13-15). To move on is to continue in the will of God. It is to realize and accept that the past life is over; live life for the now and the future. He was assuring the people that the fight belongs to God. However, the location of the army was behind the children of Israel. That was a very dangerous position.

> And when Pharaoh drew nigh, the children of Israel lifted up their eyes, and, behold, the Egyptians marched after them; and they were sore afraid: and the children of Israel cried out unto the LORD. And they said unto Moses, Because *there were* no graves in Egypt, hast thou taken us away to die in the wilderness? wherefore hast thou dealt thus with us, to carry us forth out of Egypt? *Is* not this the word that we did tell thee in Egypt, saying, Let us alone, that we may serve the Egyptians? For *it had been* better for us to serve the Egyptians, than that we should die in the wilderness. (Exodus 14:10-12)

The enemy's position was behind the Israelites. The problem that happened was the enemy was about to step into an area that God has not given them permission: "And the waters returned, and covered the chariots, and the horsemen, *and* all the host of Pharaoh that came into the sea after them; there remained not so much as one of them" (Exodus 14:28). In the book of Psalms, we know that God has set up a barrier for his children's backs. All of the army's gear in Ephesians chapter 6 only protects the front of the soldier as he going forward, because God knows He will protect the soldier's back. "Surely goodness and mercy shall follow me all the days of my life: and I will dwell in the house of the LORD for ever" (Psalm 23:6). Can you see the Devil and his evil spiritual host stepping into goodness and mercy?

Depression and praise are contradictory to each other. The book of Isaiah gives an example of this fact.

> The spirit of the Lord GOD *is* upon me; because the LORD hath anointed me to preach good tidings unto the meek; he hath sent me to bind up the brokenhearted, to proclaim liberty to the captives, and the opening of the prison to *them that are* bound; To proclaim the acceptable year of the LORD, and the day of vengeance of our God; to

> comfort all that mourn; To appoint unto them that mourn
> in Zion, to give unto them beauty for ashes, the oil of joy
> for mourning, the garment of praise for the spirit of heavi-
> ness; that they might be called trees of righteousness, the
> planting of the LORD, that he might be glorified. (Isaiah
> 61:1-3)

A garment is an article of clothing, an outer covering or outward ap-
pearances. Why a "garment of praise?" When the Devil and his host are
throwing their fiery darts, penetrating of the garment has to occur before
the individual is injured. None of the Devil's devices can reach the saint
because praise is a place in God that Satan is not allowed. Now, if the
spirit of heaviness or depression is upon someone and they feel wounded
already by the enemy, they can get the devil off of them with praise. They
can move themselves into the area of God and let the healing process
begin, stopping the enemy from completely killing them. A garment is
something a person decides to wear. One has to decide to put it on. It
is a decision, a choice given by God. Nobody can make anybody praise
God, and nobody can stop anyone from praising God, but yourself.

Deliverance Happens During Praise: All At Once

Praise brings liberty and freedom. In the early stages of the church, Paul
and Silas found themselves in a situation that only praise and prayer
helped. In the book of Acts, it records their encounter with bondage and
praise that we need to examine closely. First, we will look at their physical freedom, and then translate spiritual meaning in connection to praise.

> And it came to pass, as we went to prayer, a certain dam-
> sel possessed with a spirit of divination met us, which
> brought her masters much gain by soothsaying: The
> same followed Paul and us, and cried, saying, These men
> are the servants of the most high God, which show unto

us the way of salvation. And this did she many days. But Paul, being grieved, turned and said to the spirit, I command thee in the name of Jesus Christ to come out of her. And he came out the same hour. And when her masters saw that the hope of their gains was gone, they caught Paul and Silas, and drew *them* into the marketplace unto the rulers, And brought them to the magistrates, saying, These men, being Jews, do exceedingly trouble our city, And teach customs, which are not lawful for us to receive, neither to observe, being Romans. And the multitude rose up together against them: and the magistrates rent off their clothes, and commanded to beat *them*. And when they had laid many stripes upon them, they cast *them* into prison, charging the jailor to keep them safely: Who, having received such a charge, thrust them into the inner prison, and made their feet fast in the stocks. And at midnight Paul and Silas prayed, and sang praises unto God: and the prisoners heard them. And suddenly there was a great earthquake, so that the foundations of the prison were shaken: and immediately all the doors were opened, and every one's bands were loosed. (Acts 16:16-26)

Now let us look at this segment of scripture from a spiritual point of view. This girl was in bondage. Her masters were demons, wickedness in high places. This scripture warns us that demons know who the children of God are, and they are keeping an eye on us. The Bible said this slave girl shouted out Paul's intent for many days. She was warning sinners, that Paul was witnessing the salvation of God. In verse 18, Paul started a fight when he turned around and commanded the evil spirit to leave the young girl's body. Paul knew that God was protecting his back; he had no need to address that issue. He picked a spiritual battle with the demons that were vexing (annoying) him. Now we all know the real fight is between Satan and God, but Paul's tolerance level—or the lack thereof—was at the edge. The powers that saints have to cast out a demon in Jesus' name has become a factor in this story. Satan had to give up some territory and influence over the human race. Paul commanded the evil spirit to depart from the girl, and it obeyed him. When the demons found out they lost their power to practice their wicked scheme through this girl, the fight was on. The demons fought back, and they captured Paul and Silas and dragged them before their government officials, Satan and the demonic host, and they went to court. The evil spirits, the girl's masters, had a right to take Paul and Silas into their court because the slave girl had her right to choose what side of the battle she wanted. People are not forced to obey or love God. God wants people to love Him because they want to. Paul had violated her spiritual rights. The demons gave their arguments in their marketplace: these men being Jews, Paul and Silas are saved men of God, not from here, not part of us, are trying to change the people in our city, where we have authority. The government that saves men and women is different. Their government is one of holiness. However, Satan and his demons are subject to them [Christians] as they are submit to the will of God. First, some demonic spirits have assigned territory on the earth today. They will obey, but they will be back and will bring help to oppose us. A saved person will not agree with the customs and laws of the Devil. The Devil and demons will not receive or observe the things of God. This is why saved people and unsaved people cannot be best friends. "Be ye not unequally yoked together with unbelievers: for what fellowship hath righteousness with unrighteousness? and what communion hath light with darkness?" (2 Corinthians 6:14).

Now all these demonic spirits were in a conference, in unity against Paul and Silas. Their magistrates (the Devil) exposed Paul's and Silas' weakness (sins—Paul's anger, and taking away the girl's spiritual rights) and the demons started to attack them strongly so that the apostles would not exercise their power over them. The scripture said Paul and Silas was beaten with rods. Being beaten with rods are tests and trials in a person's area of weakness. The Devil is a dirty fighter. The demons put Paul and Silas into prison, which is bondage, depression, lack of self-esteem; things of a negative nature. The demons were trying to make Paul and Silas think that there is no hope for their situation. Then the devil has assigned a stronger demon to keep them in this state. This is call going to the next level in God. Beware; Satan also has demons on all levels that are looking for a new assignment.

The inner prison is within one's mind, called a stronghold. Strongholds are wrong things that we have done or experienced on the wrong side of the tracks in our past, or ungodly things (sins). Paul and Silas were fastened in the stocks, so they would stop exercising authority in that demonic territory. Nothing physical could get them loose, because the battle was spiritual in nature. This is a time to be still and steadfast in trusting God. These issues, one's personal strongholds, have to be dealt with before you can go to the next level.

This is how freedom occurs. Midnight represents the lowest and darkest times of one's life. When a person makes up their mind to overcome these issues, that point in time is their midnight, is called the turning point. This struggle is personal. You cannot help anybody to obtain his or her freedom. The first thing Paul and Silas did was pray and sing. They had a conversation with God, and then they gave Him some praise and honor to show God that they still trust Him. No matter what situation life finds you in, praise God. They were Shabaching, to address God in a loud tone. How do we know they were loud? Because the prisoners, all of the strongholds were listening; this is the key. Singing during praise and worship services brings God to you. "But thou *art* holy, O *thou* that inhabitest the praises of Israel" (Psalm 22:3). To inhabit is "to occupy as a place of settled residence or habitat: live in "Now the Lord is that Spirit: and where the Spirit of the Lord *is*, there *is* liberty [freedom]" (2 Corinthians 3:17).

Along with obedience, listening is part of the key to deliverance. First, praises make the enemy shut up, and God comes to you. Hearing the Word of God is possible. Praise binds the kings and nobles and anything that is not godly; we have to put fetters of iron on them in the spiritual realm. Then when the saints are ministering to God, the Devil cannot interrupt. During worship, one is seeking God to pick them up out of their situations (Towdah). Then a time of atonement with God happens. One has a chance to tell God they believe His report. God's report is that there is hope for one's situation.

"And **suddenly** there was a great earthquake, so that the foundations of the prison were shaken: and immediately all the doors were opened, and every one's bands were loosed" (Acts 16:26). Suddenly is how fast God responds to praise—you do not have to wait. The violent earthquake represents God busting into the situation, His word coming alive, which brings freedom and peace. When an earthquake happens in one's life, everyone has knowledge about it. An earthquake brings about a change that people can plainly see. The foundation is referring to the very root of a problem or situation. All of the stones will be turned at once. All the doors were opened; that means all of one's strongholds are addressed at once. Therefore, it does not matter how many problems or situations a person is facing. All of them can be resolved at once. A complete healing can occur all at once.

There are thousands of benefits of praise, but only three were analyzed. First, praise makes the enemies shut up. Second, praise neutralizes depression. Third, deliverance can occur during praise. Praise is lifting up God. Humanity also has a great deal to gain in the process. These spiritual benefits are worth more than money. Spiritual healing can solve spiritual and physical problems.

Praise is a very powerful force. People today are battling with a variety of situations that can only be solved on the spiritual level. When praise makes the enemy shut up, one can hear the Word of God. His Word is a healing force, nutrients for a person's soul. God speaks softly and calmly. A person has to pay attention on purpose to hear the message. Praise neutralizes depression. Depression is like acid. Acid has the power to burn up anything that comes in contact with it. So, when a person is depressed, that situation that they dealing with is burning their life at that moment. Now, praise is a base that takes acid and makes it useless. Once the burning stops, healing can take place. Praise brings deliverance now. God lives in the presence of true and acceptable praise. Everything that is good and holy can be accomplished in the presence of God.

Chapter Five

Distinguishing Praise and Worship

Driving up and down the street, passing church after church, they all have signs posted saying, **Praise and Worship Service**; afterward, the day and time is posted. How are these two words interrelated to each other? Praise and worship service is not a time to ask God for anything that is called prayer. Praise and worship are their meaning interchangeable, or are they different? A Christian life can demonstrate both if they are striving toward their potential. Praise and worship are a Christian lifestyle not only for Sunday morning service events. Praise should take place every day. Everybody can and should give God praise. However, can everybody enter into worship? The Holy Bible illustrates several clear-cut examples of worship.

Praise

We defined praise in Chapter one. Praise "is an expression (physical and vocal) of heartfelt gratitude and thanksgiving to God for all that he has done or will do for us." Everybody and every living thing that has breath is capable of giving God praise. "Let every thing that hath breath praise the LORD. Praise ye the LORD" (Psalm 150:6). Praise is performing collectively or alone to get God's attention as one enters the gates in the spiritual realm. In the physical, people are in the church, but in the spiritual realm, they enter the gates of God's throne with praise. In a praise service, people are reminding, talking, singing, and expressing God's goodness to those around them and/or to themselves. In most of the praise songs, people are talking to each other about God. Praise takes that individual into the realization of whom God is.

Worship

Worship is the "reverent honor and homage paid to God." Worship is the highest form of praise. In worship, a person expresses their admiration of God Himself for His personality, character, attributes, and perfection. In worship, a person is ministering to God for who He is and not just for what He has done for them. To minister is when "a person acts as an agent or instrument of another or themselves by speaking hope and faith in God." Who is God? God is a Healer, Peace, Friend, Creator, Lover, Savior, Author and Finisher of our Faith, Judge, Revenger, Joy, Forgiver, Provider, Banner, etc. During praise service, physical by nature, people are seeking God's attention. However, when this contact is accomplished, the focus shifts from praise to worship; the individual is now ministering to God. Worship is when a person approaches God in a one-on-one personal confrontation, master-to-creation relationship. Worship is talking or singing to God. It is a spontaneous overflow of these thoughts and emotions of God's existence. KEY: Only saved (born again) people can worship God.

God has specific requirements that people have to observe in order to worship Him. Let us look at the example of Moses coming for the first time to worship God.

> And Moses said, I will now turn aside, and see this great sight, why the bush is not burnt. And when the LORD saw that he turned aside to see, God called unto him out of the midst of the bush, and said, Moses, Moses. And he said, Here *am* I. And he said, Draw not nigh hither: put off thy shoes from off thy feet, for the place whereon thou

standest *is* holy ground. .... And he said, Certainly I will be with thee; and this *shall be* a token unto thee, that I have sent thee: When thou hast brought forth the people out of Egypt, ye shall serve God upon this mountain. (Exodus 3:3-5, 12)

We need to look at the scripture on a spiritual level. In Exodus 3:3, Moses said, "I will now turn." The word **turn** shows that when someone comes to God, turning is required. A change has to occur, in the direction toward what God calls holiness. All of humanity is born in sin; therefore, turning has occurred in all worshipers' lives in order to approach God. Next, verse 4 "when the LORD saw that he turned." God, not people, knows when a person's inner change has occurred. Only then, God will react to a praiser. Then, verse 5 says, "draw not nigh hither" God has requirements before entering into His presence. Now what about the **shoes**? God told Moses, "put off thy shoes from thy feet." Moses was wearing shoes that symbolize his past life. Our shoes represent where we have been or our current state of being. Taking off the shoes means that people cannot just walk into the presence of God any kind of way. God demands respect and honor. People are guilty of all kinds of things because of the evidence left on their shoes. Taking off the shoes means a person is about to take a new path.

Unacceptable Worship

Some people think they can separate their praise and worship lifestyles from their daily activities. Can a person act any kind of way and worship God? Will God receive their worship? No. Living a life of holiness is required. To offer something to God that He did not ordain (establish) is called unacceptable worship. God has told us how to worship. If worship is not done right, it can cost you your life. In the Old Testament, some priest lost their lives physically. A person's spiritual gifts or positions in the church organization do not dictate that God will accept their worship.

Here is the account of Aaron's two sons, who were priests unto God with their unacceptable worship.

> And Nadab and Abihu, the sons of Aaron, took either of them his censer, and put fire therein, and put incense thereon, and offered strange fire before the LORD, which he commanded them not. And there went out fire from the LORD, and devoured them, and they died before the LORD. (Leviticus 10:1, 2)

Some people might not die physically, but they die in the spiritual realm. Another example of unacceptable worship involved Cain. The offering that Cain gave did not satisfy God, because Cain decided to give God what he wanted to offer Him.

> And in process of time it came to pass, that Cain brought of the fruit of the ground an offering unto the LORD.... And the LORD said unto Cain, Why art thou wroth? and why is thy countenance fallen? If thou doest well, shalt thou not be accepted? and if thou doest not well, sin lieth at the door. And unto thee *shall be* his desire, and thou shalt rule over him. (Genesis 4:3, 6, 7)

In order for God to accept praise and worship, the heart of the worshiper must be right. The heart of a person is what God is seeking. Anyone can demonstrate the outer expression of praise and worship. In the New Testament, Jesus taught about unacceptable worship: "This people draweth nigh unto me with their mouth, and honoureth me with *their* lips; but their heart is far from me. But in vain they do worship me, teaching *for* doctrines the commandments of men" (Matthew 15:8, 9). The word vain means "without success." Therefore, their worship was a waste of time and energy that profited them nothing. God is seeking true worshipers. Every time a person lifts their hands, shouts

Hallelujah, dances, speaks in tongues, it does not mean anything unless the heart of the individual is in the right relationship with God. God said, He is holy and we are to be holy. Holiness is a standard of the relationship that He has ordained. To be holy is an easy concept; just obey God in everything. "And the LORD spake unto Moses, saying, Speak unto all the congregation of the children of Israel, and say unto them, Ye shall be holy: for I the LORD your God *am* holy" (Leviticus 19:1, 2).

Acceptable Worship

Worship is an outward expression of an inward devotion toward God, one of obedience and submission. Worship is the time of coming into atonement with God. Why is making an atonement to God important? What is atonement? To be in atonement is to come into agreement, oneness with God. It is not a temporary state of being; it is a lasting position. An atonement places one in the position in which God has created man from the beginning. Man was created and given power and dominion over everything on earth. Atonement restores man to his proper place, the head, and the leader, one of authority and control. Atonement is to enter agreement with and operate in God's Will. In the Old Testament, the priest had to offer a blood sacrifice unto God to ask for the forgiveness of sin. Sin breaks the bonds of the atonement state, therefore, shifting man from his proper place. Sin is the wedge that breaks the bond of atonement between man and God; therefore, placing man' authority out of control.

This is how the atonement process works. "And the priest shall make an atonement for him before the LORD: and it shall be forgiven him for any thing of all that he hath done in trespassing therein" (Leviticus 6:7). Now the priest was to wash his physical body with water. They were to clean themselves before putting on holy clothes to come before God. In addition, they brought an offering in their hands that God had chosen. They did not enter the presence of God empty handed. In the book of

Leviticus, God gave Moses instruction on how a priest is to enter His presence.

> And the LORD spake unto Moses after the death of the two sons of Aaron, when they offered before the LORD, and died; And the LORD said unto Moses, Speak unto Aaron thy brother, that he come not at all times into the holy *place* within the veil before the mercy seat, which *is* upon the ark; that he die not: for I will appear in the cloud upon the mercy seat. Thus shall Aaron come into the holy *place*: with a young bullock for a sin offering, and a ram for a burnt offering. He shall put on the holy linen coat, and he shall have the linen breeches upon his flesh, and shall be girded with a linen girdle, and with the linen mitre shall he be attired: these *are* holy garments; therefore shall he wash his flesh in water, and *so* put them on. (Leviticus 16:1-4)

Now the New Testament will give the spiritual meaning behind this scripture. In addition, in the book of Ephesians, a clearer detail of a priest approach unto God is shown. Chapter Six discusses the priesthood in more detail.

> Husbands, love your wives, even as Christ also loved the church, and gave himself for it; That he might sanctify and cleanse it with the washing of water by the word, That he might present it to himself a glorious church, not having spot, or wrinkle, or any such thing; but that it should be holy and without blemish. (Ephesians 5:25-27)

Jesus Christ has given himself and his blood as a sin offering for humanity. He has given a perfect sacrifice that never needs repeating. The priest washing their body with water represents us washing our inner man with the Word of God. During the washing process, one is ridding oneself of sin, unrighteousness, and anything that is not like God. God's Word is the sword that cuts all impurities away—spots, wrinkles and blemishes—in the spiritual realm. A Christian is to be without spot, wrinkle or blemish. A **wrinkle** is a temporary slight ridge or furrow (a marked narrow depression, a deep wrinkle) on a surface. An example of a wrinkle is a little white lie, occasional gossip, blue moon dirt movie, a weekend party with alcoholic drinks, and selfish ambition, just to name a few. A **spot** is a rounded mark or stain by foreign matter, not Godly, somewhat like mud, or sin. A spot in a fabric has a texture differed from the original texture. A spot is normally round and grows outward. The danger in a spot is that it spread in all areas of a person life. A **blemish** diminishes the perfection of an object. A blemish is like the wrinkle has grown to a spot, and now that sin is a part of a person's lifestyle. A blemish usually happens when a person has impurity, underneath and all of a sudden, they reveal themselves. A blemish destroys the relationship between God and man. God cannot dwell in that atmosphere. These issues must be dealt with in order to have acceptable worship. "But the hour cometh, and now is, when the true worshippers shall worship the Father in spirit and in truth: for the Father seeketh such to worship him. God *is* a Spirit: and they that worship him must worship *him* in spirit and in truth" (John 4:23, 24).

A true worshiper is a person who worships God "in spirit and truth." The Spirit of truth is the Holy Spirit that enters into the heart of a Christian when they give their life to God. John 14:15-17 expresses this point; Jesus was talking to his disciples.

If ye love me, keep my commandments. And I will pray the Father, and he shall give you another Comforter, that he may abide with you for ever; *Even* the Spirit of truth; whom the world cannot receive, because it seeth him not, neither knoweth him: but ye know him; for he dwelleth with you, and shall be in you.

After Jesus' death, Peter continues this same massage.

> Then Peter said unto them, Repent, and be baptized every
> one of you in the name of Jesus Christ for the remission of
> sins, and ye shall receive the gift of the Holy Ghost. (Acts
> 2:38)

A person who has not given their life to God does not have the Spirit
of Truth; therefore, they are incapable of true worship. Their minds are
carnal by nature and hostile, "an enemy" towards God. To have a carnal
mind means that a person depends on the fleshly senses or body, their
passions and appetites, in making judgments. The book of Romans and
Corinthians explain the mind of a sinner.

> Because the carnal mind *is* enmity [hostile] against God:
> for it is not subject to the law of God, neither indeed can
> be. So then they that are in the flesh cannot please God.
> (Romans 8:7, 8)

> But the natural man receiveth not the things of the Spirit
> of God: for they are foolishness [stupid, senseless] unto
> him: neither can he know *them*, because they are spiritu-
> ally discerned [detected]. (1 Corinthians 2:14)

Worship Begins at Home

Worship begins with an individual at home alone or with family. Worship
is a lifestyle of obedience to God in all areas in one's life. All who worship
God have to make a change in their life at one time or another.

> Now therefore fear the LORD, and serve him in sincer-
> ity and in truth: and put away the gods which your fa-
> thers served on the other side of the flood, and in Egypt;

and serve ye the LORD. And if it seem evil unto you to serve the LORD, choose you this day whom ye will serve; whether the gods which your fathers served that *were* on the other side of the flood, or the gods of the Amorites, in whose land ye dwell: but as for me and my house, we will serve the LORD. (Joshua 24:14, 15)

Here we have Joshua talking to all the tribes of Israel—elders, leaders, judges and officials. The focus in this book is on what he said at the end, "me and my household." As the head of the house, he took authority and responsibility for the leadership that God has given him. God has given the leadership of the family to the husband. The husband (head of the house) is responsible for the spiritual well-being of the family unto God. There is no reason why men should go to church and allow anybody in their household to remain at home; women whose husbands do not go to church, this responsibility falls upon you. You are the priest. God has commanded parents to train your child in the way of the Lord. Question, when does your child stop being your child? Never, but as long as that child is under your roof, you should exercise your authority as the priest unto God in that child life. If your children are not under your roof, allow your conversations or opinion to be based on the word of God.

Churches today have Sunday morning service, Sunday school, Children's Church, Youth Church, Bible Study and Revival. The church has provided many avenues to help children to learn how to live a Godly life. The churches provide these good services. Now it is not wrong for churches to help in this growing and needed task; however, God has a plan of His own. God's plan is that parents and grandparents are to teach their children. This responsibility has not been changed. God has pointed out that teaching takes place all day long, not just forty-five minutes to an hour and a half twice a week at church. Here are three scriptures instructing parents and grandparents to educated their children and grandchildren about God and how to live a godly life.

Only take heed to thyself, and keep thy soul diligently, lest thou forget the things which thine eyes have seen, and lest they depart from thy heart all the days of thy life: but teach them thy sons, and thy sons' sons. (Deuteronomy 4:9)

Therefore shall ye lay up these my words in your heart and in your soul, and bind them for a sign upon your hand, that they may be as frontlets between your eyes. And ye shall teach them your children, speaking of them when thou sittest in thine house, and when thou walkest by the way, when thou liest down, and when thou risest up. And thou shalt write them upon the door posts of thine house, and upon thy gates. (Deuteronomy 11:18-20)

Let the deacons be the husbands of one wife, ruling their children and their own houses well. (1 Timothy 3:12)

In summary, praise and worship are different. These words are not interchangeable. The Bible has given a clear-cut explanation of true worship. It has been established that every living thing that has breath can and should give God the creator praise. However, only Spirit-filled, born again people can enter into worship. Finally, the responsibility of children's education about God still lies in the hands of their parents and grandparents. No matter how good of a service a church provides with its education, this task has not passed to the hands of the church.

Chapter Six

Understanding the Priesthood

What is a priest? And what is a priesthood? What are the qualifications of a priest and who establishes their existence? When did the priesthood start? Why and how is a priest connected with praise and worship? Does the priesthood still exist? Who is the high priest now, and what significance does he represent? All believers in Christ need to understand the roles, history, changes, and significances of the priesthood and the office of the High Priest. Are you a priest? At the end of this chapter, you should be able to answer these questions with confidence and accuracy.

The Origin of the Priesthood

The word priest means one who is an ordained person who does "religious rites to make sacrificial offerings." A priest offers serves (work) to the one they obey. At first, God dealt with man one-on- one: Abraham, Isaac, Jacob. Jacob had so many children, a nation began; God established a plan to deal with a large group of people. He had intended that all men and women to be a priest from the beginning. This promise of being priests was for the whole twelve tribes of Israel to be a kingdom of priest unto God; however, just the tribe of Levi received that position until Christ's death. Here is the encounter that happened after the children of Israel had fled from Egypt.

> Now therefore, if ye will obey my voice indeed, and keep my covenant, then ye shall be a peculiar treasure unto me above all people: for all the earth *is* mine: And ye shall be unto me a kingdom of priests, and an holy nation. These *are* the words which thou shalt speak unto the children of Israel.... And all the people answered together, and said, All that the LORD hath spoken we will do. And Moses returned the words of the people unto the LORD. (Exodus 19:5, 6, 8)

To seal the deal that God had made with the twelve tribes of Israel, it was necessary to sign the agreement in blood. Blood is the life of flesh (Leviticus 17:11). Moses took blood of an ox and sprinkled it on the altar and the people, and the first covenant [Mosaic Covenant] came to life.

> And he sent young men of the children of Israel, which offered burnt offerings, and sacrificed peace offerings of oxen unto the LORD. And Moses took half of the blood, and put *it* in basins; and half of the blood he sprinkled on the altar. And he took the book of the covenant, and read in the audience of the people: and they said, All that the LORD hath said will we do, and be obedient. And Moses took the blood, and sprinkled *it* on the people, and said, Behold the blood of the covenant, which the LORD hath made with you concerning all these words. (Exodus 24:5-8)

However, only the tribe of Levi, Leah's and Jacob's third son entered and walked into this promise of priesthood in the Mosaic Covenant. Levi and his brother Simeon were very violent men by nature. Jacob described their behavior as angry, cruel, and fierce. Their father feared their nature, so upon his death he dispersed these two tribes (Levi and Simeon) into the other ten tribes of Israel. This was good, because if outsiders decided to attack, these two dispersed groups of people would be ready to fight. This is how the tribe of Levi received the blessing of being priests and the priesthood from God.

> And when the people saw that Moses delayed to come down out of the mount, the people gathered themselves together unto Aaron, and said unto him, Up, make us gods, which shall go before us; for *as for* this Moses, the man that brought us up out of the land of Egypt, we wot not what is become of him..... And when Moses saw that the people *were* naked; (for Aaron had made them naked unto *their* shame among their enemies:) Then Moses stood in the gate of the camp, and said, Who *is* on the LORD'S side? *let him come* unto me. And all the sons of Levi gathered themselves together unto him. And he said unto them, Thus saith the LORD God of Israel, Put every man his sword by his side, *and* go in and out from gate to gate throughout the camp, and slay every man his brother, and every man his companion, and every man his neighbour. And the children of Levi did according to the word of Moses: and there fell of the people that day about three thousand men. For Moses had said, Consecrate yourselves to day to the LORD, even every man upon his son, and upon his brother; that he may bestow upon you a blessing this day. (Exodus 32:1, 25-29)

To be set apart in this scripture means to consecrate, "to make or declare sacredly, to be anointed" or to be "dedicated for the service of a deity." Here the deity is the Supreme Being, God. Choosing righteous over unrighteousness God has a blessing in store for that individual that day. Why did God choose the tribe of Levi to receive the priesthood in the Old Testament? He did not choose the tribe of Levi; the tribe of Levi chose Him. When all the Israelites were given a choice to choose what God one will serve and be willing to kill those ties that were not associated with God, only the tribe of Levi stepped up to the plate. The Levi chose God and obeyed Him, and therefore they received the blessing—the office of High priest and priesthood as an inheritance. God had to have a reason for choosing the Levi because God is not a respecter of people, but He is a respecter of principles. Even Peter said, "Then Peter opened *his* mouth, and said, Of a truth I perceive that God is no respecter of persons: But in every nation he that feareth him, and worketh righteousness, is accepted with him" (Acts 10:34, 35). Now, people today have to kill every relationship with brother, friend, and neighbor who persists in idolatry and immorality, and issues that come between them and God. Some things God expects people to do for themselves, such as removing obstacles that block one's way to Him. This is why the tribe of Levi held the office of High priest and priesthood in the first [Mosaic] covenant.

To be a priest was and is an honor and a privilege. It is important that priests know and obey the instructions of God as they come to offer praises and worship. God has outlined how to appear unto Him. A priest must not come carelessly, disobedient, with a desire to do his own will, or according to the world's traditions. The world is anything or anyone who is not in line with the Word of God. One must take care that songs, music, and customs of this world or from ungodly religious practices do not creep into the worship service. It will be characterized as "unauthorized worship," just like what Aaron's sons did. That unauthorized worship cost them their lives. Aaron's sons knew how to enter the presence of God, but they purposely disobeyed the rules. It is not permissible for priests to carry their personal selfish sorrows into the presence of God (Leviticus 10:3-7).

The other eleven tribes of Israel were not ready to enter the priesthood of God. Their sins have held them back. The prophet Hosea gives an insight on why some of the Israelites did not enter into the priesthood. God said,

> My people are destroyed for lack of knowledge: because thou hast rejected knowledge, I will also reject thee, that thou shalt be no priest to me: seeing thou hast forgotten the law of thy God, I will also forget thy children. (Hosea 4:6)

Characteristics of a Priest

There are a few characteristics of a priest. First, a priest must be <u>set apart,</u> to live a life of God's standard of holiness. "Love not the world, neither the things *that are* in the world. If any man love the world, the love of the Father is not in him" (1 John 2:15). A priest's conversation and mind should be clean, their dressing/grooming acceptable unto God, unlike the world. There are only two kingdoms, the kingdom of God and the kingdom of Darkness, Darkness, called the world. The world—this is not in reference to the physical, material world, but the invisible spiritual system of evil under the enemy control, Satan and all that it offers in opposition to God, His Word, and His people. "And let the priests also, which come near to the LORD, sanctify themselves, lest the LORD break forth upon them" (Exodus 19:22).

Second, a priest has to be <u>ordained</u>, not by man, but by God. The word ordained means "to establish or order by appointment, decree, or law." Just like God has chosen the Levi to minister unto Him, he has also chosen us in the New Covenant to minister to Him. Ephesians 1:4, 5 reads, "According as he hath chosen us in him before the foundation of the world, that we should be holy and without blame before him in love: Having predestinated us unto the adoption of children by Jesus Christ to himself, according to the good pleasure of his will." Therefore, before the creation of the world, independent of human influence and apart from human merits those who are saved have become eternally united with Christ.

Third, a priest has to <u>go through God's customized process</u> (molding) that was specially ordered for them. All priests minister unto God. They all have a job—a spiritual gift or two which requires Godly training and teaching with God as the teacher. The customize process is explained in Jeremiah chapter 18. The prophet Jeremiah gives detailed accounts of how God makes His children into the image that pleases Him. What makes the clay soft and supple to work with is repenting, turning away from sin, and walking in the way of God.

> Then I went down to the potter's house, and, behold, he wrought a work on the wheels. And the vessel that he made of clay was marred in the hand of the potter: so he made it again another vessel, as seemed good to the potter to make *it*. Then the word of the LORD came to me, saying, O house of Israel, cannot I do with you as this potter? saith the LORD. Behold, as the clay *is* in the potter's hand, so *are* ye in mine hand, O house of Israel. (Jeremiah 18:3-6)

Fourth, a priest <u>spiritually cleans themselves daily</u>. Repentance, prayer, forgiveness, and obedience—this is the prescription of spiritual cleaning. God instructed Moses to wash Aaron and his sons before they could come into his presence. "And thou shalt bring Aaron and his sons unto the door of the tabernacle of the congregation, and wash them with water" (Exodus 40:12). This is in the physical realm, and is temporary and has to be repeated. Only the exterior of the man is clean, what people see. Now, in the New Covenant, priests are to wash in the spiritual realm with an everlasting cleansing of the inner man that God examine. Prayer is a cleaning agent for all priests. "If we confess our sins, he is faithful and just to forgive us *our* sins, and to cleanse us from all unrighteousness" (I John 1:9). Also, "Repent ye therefore, and be converted, that your sins may be blotted out, when the times of refreshing shall come from the presence of the Lord" (Acts 3:19). Forgiveness unto others helps one to receive forgiveness from God. Jesus was instructing the disciples in prayer, and the subject of forgiveness came up.

> For if ye forgive men their trespasses, your heavenly Father
> will also forgive you: But if ye forgive not men their tres-
> passes, neither will your Father forgive your trespasses.
> (Matthew 6:14, 15)

Another spiritual cleaning agent is obedience. This cleaning agent is cut and dry. Right out of his own mouth, Jesus said these words, "If ye love me, keep my commandments" (John 14:15).

Our Priestly Function: Making a Connection

People go to church to meet God. When they meet God, He will take care of all of their needs. God's name is Wonderful Counselor, Healer, Provider, the Lord our Banner, Prince of Peace, etc. Whatever is bothering a wor-shiper when they meet God, their issues are automatically transferred, and the power of God that neutralizes negative forces in one's life occurs. If this does not happen, then there is a lack of faith or alignment on the be-half of the worshiper. Now, if God takes care of all of His children's needs, why did He give priests to the children of Israel? A closer look at the role of a priest will help in explaining their importance. This section will give a brief history of some functions of a priest.

> And I have taken the Levites for all the firstborn of the
> children of Israel. And I have given the Levites *as* a gift to
> Aaron and to his sons from among the children of Israel, to
> do the service of the children of Israel in the tabernacle of
> the congregation, and to make an atonement for the chil-
> dren of Israel: that there be no plague among the children
> of Israel, when the children of Israel come nigh unto the
> sanctuary. (Numbers 8:18, 19)

God has given the Levites two important jobs: the work of the temple to the tribe of Levi (priest) and to make atonement for the children of

Israel was the job of the house of Aaron (the High priest of the land). The word atonement means to reconcile between God and humanity. The final atonement was accomplished through the life, suffering, and death of Jesus Christ. The Latin word priest means pontafex (path-maker), a bridge builder. A bridge helps a person to cross over from one side to the other side. The priest was to win over, to bring into agreement or harmony, to restore the people of God to God. The High Priest was the only one that was permitted to enter the Holy of Holies in order to make atonement for the people once a year. "For on that day [Day of Atonement] shall *the priest* make an atonement for you, to cleanse you, *that* ye may be clean from all your sins before the LORD" (Leviticus 16:30). A bridge is not a one-way path. The bridge builder (priest) and God can use the bridge. God will not come unless He is invited. When God comes to see someone, they have to prepare a way for Him with praise and worship. This whole business of bridge building is personal in the New Covenant. Each bridge is personally built with one traveler on each side. People are not allowed to use anyone else's bridge. The book of Philippians makes this point clear, "Wherefore, my beloved, as ye have always obeyed, not as in my presence only, but now much more in my absence, work out your own salvation with fear and trembling"

(2:12). There is something in life that people have to do for themselves. Atonement is so important because as the Bible says, "Can two walk together, except they be agreed?" (Amos 3:3). Prayer, forgiveness, praise, and worship are all elements of building a bridge. The job of the priest is still the same. In the New Covenant, a priest builds a bridge to meet with God for themselves.

Another duty of the priest is to <u>keep the fires burning.</u>

> Command Aaron and his sons, saying, This *is* the law of the burnt offering: It *is* the burnt offering, because of the burning upon the altar all night unto the morning, and the fire of the altar shall be burning in it. ... And the fire upon

the altar shall be burning in it; it shall not be put out: and the priest shall burn wood on it every morning, and lay the burnt offering in order upon it; and he shall burn thereon the fat of the peace offerings. The fire shall ever be burning upon the altar; it shall never go out. (Leviticus 6:9, 12, 13)

The word "hearth" means the lowest section of a blast furnace, the bottom of a refinery, home, a vital or creative center. As priests, we should allow God to burn out all of the sins down to the foundations or the roots of their existence in our lives. In the New Covenant, in the book of Romans, the offering to be placed on the burning altar is the priest themselves in the spiritual realm. Romans 12:1 says to the children of God, "I beseech you therefore, brethren, by the mercies of God, that ye present your bodies a living sacrifice, holy, acceptable unto God, *which is* your reasonable service." As a priest, one has a commitment unto God to keep a (perpetual) continuous fire burning. The Mosaic Covenant operated under the physical temporary realm, but the New Covenant operates under the spiritual permanent realm. The fire should be on the hearth—home (personal), the bottom of a refinery, to burn at the foundation or the root of sins in that person's life. A priest is command to burn fat on the altar in the presence of God. Fat is the part of an animal that holds toxins—poisons, impurities in that animal. Question: What fat did you put on the altar this morning? On the other hand, priests are you putting your fat upon the altar daily? Keeping a continuously burning altar means that as priests, we are daily cleaning our spiritual man until our change comes.

The third part of the process of making atonement is to <u>clear out the ashes</u> from the altar. A fire cannot continue to burn if the ashes are permitted to accumulate. As for those impurities that the priest laid on the altar, after they are consumed by fire, the priest is responsible for getting rid of their ashes.

> And the priest shall put on his linen garment, and his linen breeches shall he put upon his flesh, and take up the ashes which the fire hath consumed with the burnt offering on the altar, and he shall put them beside the altar. And he shall put off his garments, and put on other garments, and carry forth the ashes without the camp unto a clean place. (Leviticus 6:10, 11)

Memories of the past impurity will smother the fire for the future. Priests must be willing to leave the past, both good and bad experiences, if they are to run and not faint.

Fourth, a priest has to <u>offer sacrifices</u>. When the children of God were to gather in the sight of God, they were told not to be empty handed. A token of financial gratification was required. The things they offered were physical in nature because the Mosaic Covenant was founded on physical promises.

> Three times in a year shall all thy males appear before the LORD thy God in the place which he shall choose; in the feast of unleavened bread, and in the feast of weeks, and in the feast of tabernacles: and they shall not appear before the LORD empty: Every man *shall give* as he is able, according to the blessing of the LORD thy God which he hath given thee. (Deuteronomy 16:16, 17)

> Will a man rob God? Yet ye have robbed me. But ye say, Wherein have we robbed thee? In tithes and offerings. Ye *are* cursed with a curse: for ye have robbed me, *even* this whole nation. Bring ye all the tithes into the storehouse, that there may be meat in mine house, and prove me now herewith, saith the LORD of hosts, if I will not open you the windows of heaven, and pour you out a blessing, that

there shall not *be room* enough *to receive it.* (Malachi 3:8-10)

Honour the LORD with thy substance, and with the first-fruits [to reestablish, to bring back] of all thine increase. (Proverbs 3:9)

In the New Covenant, the priests are to offer spiritual things. "By him therefore let us offer the sacrifice of praise to God continually, that is, the fruit of *our* lips giving thanks to his name" (Hebrews 13:15). They are to thank God for purifying their lives.

Fifth, a priest should <u>speak blessing upon the children of God.</u>

And the LORD spake unto Moses, saying, Speak unto Aaron and unto his sons, saying, On this wise ye shall bless the children of Israel, saying unto them, The LORD bless thee, and keep thee: The LORD make his face shine upon thee, and be gracious unto thee: The LORD lift up his countenance upon thee, and give thee peace. And they shall put my name upon the children of Israel; and I will bless them. (Numbers 6:22-27)

Priests are to speak blessings into each other's lives. Jesus, our High Priest, spoke blessings into the children of God's lives in the book of Matthew chapter five. Speaking blessings into a person's life is like saying positive truth that God has in store for His people through His will. God gives those blessings after the priest speaks them. A Priest can speak blessing into your wife's, husband's, and children's lives. "Death and life *are* in the power of the tongue: and they that love it shall eat the fruit thereof" (Proverbs 18:21). Listen. What are you speaking?

In conclusion, the priest has at least five functions. One, the priest is a bridge builder that makes a connection to God to obtain atonement for sins. Second, a priest has to keep a fire continually burning on the altar. This will allow the fat (impurity) to burn out of one's life; also reminding one that repentance, prayer, forgiveness and obedience are daily and continuous activities of the priest. Third, a priest gets rid of the past sins (memories, old contacts, partners in crime). Fourth, a priest is to offer sacrifices of praises unto God. Fifth, a priest speaks blessings unto themselves and the children of God.

Why a Change in the Covenant and Priesthood

The word covenant means, "A formal agreement, between two or more persons to do or not to do something specified." In addition, covenant means a "conditional promise made to humanity by God as revealed in Scripture." In the book of Exodus after the children of Israel came out of Egypt, God met with them at Mount Sinai. God declared unto them that they will be "a kingdom of priest and an holy nation" unto Him (Exodus 19:6). When God entered into this First Covenant (Mosaic Covenant), blood was used to seal the deal. The blood was sprinkled on all the people and on the scroll. Therefore, they had entered into a binding blood agreement. In the scripture, the book of Hebrews 9:19, 20 explains this point.

> For when Moses had spoken every precept to all the people according to the law, he took the blood of calves and of goats, with water, and scarlet wool, and hyssop, and sprinkled both the book, and all the people, Saying, This *is* the blood of the testament which God hath enjoined unto you.

Part of Jesus' mission was to fulfill the scriptures Matthew 5:17. To fulfill means to bring to an end and to convert into reality. The Lord's Passover teaches us how the priesthood changes from the physical to spiritual, from the Mosaic Covenant and priesthood to the New Covenant and priesthood, from the Old High Priests to the New High Priest, from the temporary agreement to a everlasting agreement. The first Passover happened in Egypt when the Israelites were in bondage and God was going to allow his angels to kill the entire first born of humans and beasts in the land. However, the angels were ordered to Passover the houses that had blood on them.

> Your lamb shall be without blemish, a male of the first year: ye shall take *it* out from the sheep, or from the goats: And ye shall keep it up until the fourteenth day of the same month: and the whole assembly of the congregation of Israel shall kill it in the evening. And they shall take of the blood, and strike *it* on the two side posts and on the upper door post of the houses, wherein they shall eat it. ....
> For I will pass through the land of Egypt this night, and will smite all the firstborn in the land of Egypt, both man and beast; and against all the gods of Egypt I will execute judgment: I *am* the LORD. And the blood shall be to you for a token upon the houses where ye *are*: and when I see the blood, I will pass over you, and the plague shall not be upon you to destroy *you*, when I smite the land of Egypt. (Exodus 12:5-7, 12, 13)

This passage of scripture will be explained bit by bit; by the end of this chapter, a full picture of the transferring of the covenant and the priesthood will be fully made clear.

There are several reasons why a New Covenant is necessary. First, God said that He has "found fault with the people" concerning the [Mosaic] First Covenant. A fault is "an error or mistake." The first covenant's principles were external by nature. The laws of God were written on tablets, the blood of goats and bulls was sprinkled on the people, which brought about an outwardly cleaning, a "show." The blood sprinkled on the people was "not able to clear the conscience of the worshiper" (Hebrews 9:1, 9, 10).

> Then verily the first *covenant* [Mosaic Covenant] had also ordinances of divine service, and a worldly sanctuary... Which *was* a figure for the time then present, in which were offered both gifts and sacrifices, that could not make him that did the service perfect, as pertaining to the conscience; *Which stood* only in meats and drinks, and divers washings, and carnal ordinances, imposed *on them* until the time of reformation.

A New Covenant with Israel and the house of Judah was establish by God. The agreement with the house of Israel was that God was going to write his laws in their minds. The conscience, "the inner sense of what is right or wrong in one conduct or motives," or "the moral principles that control or inhibit the actions or thoughts of an individual" is what God's main purpose was in making a new covenant. When Jesus offered the cup of wine to his disciples, he referred to it as the blood of the new covenant. The blood was to be **ingested internally** for an internal change. God also found fault with the Levitical priesthood. The Levitical system did not provide any direct contact into God's presence for His people. Rather, it kept them out.

> If therefore perfection were by the Levitical priesthood, (for under it the people received the law,) what further need *was there* that another priest should rise after the order of Melchisedec, and not be called after the order of Aaron? For the priesthood being changed, there is made of necessity a change also of the law. For he of whom these things are spoken pertaineth to another tribe, of which no man gave attendance at the altar. For *it is* evident that

our Lord sprang out of Juda; of which tribe Moses spake
nothing concerning priesthood. (Hebrews 7:11-14)

The new agreement God made with the house of Judah was to make
Jesus a High Priest in the order of Melchizedek in order to offer one perfect blood sacrifice for all of humanity for the remission of sin. "How
much more shall the blood of Christ, who through the eternal Spirit offered himself without spot to God, purge your conscience from dead
works to serve the living God?" (Hebrews 9:14). Jesus' priesthood is
permanent, because he lives forever. "Wherefore he is able also to save
them to the uttermost that come unto God by him, seeing he ever liveth
to make intercession for them. For such an high priest became us, *who
is* holy, harmless, undefiled, separate from sinners, and made higher than
the heavens" (Hebrews 7:25, 26).

Why a change in the covenant and a new priesthood? Because,
Christ's offering was a one-for-all sacrifice which was superior to all the
sacrifices of the Levitical system.

When the Changes Occurred

Jesus, when he had cried again with a loud voice, yielded up the ghost. And, behold, the veil of the temple was
rent in twain from the top to the bottom; and the earth did
quake, and the rocks rent. (Matthew 27:50, 51)

But when they came to Jesus, and saw that he was dead
already, they brake not his legs: But one of the soldiers
with a spear pierced his side, and forthwith came there
out blood and water. (John 19:33, 34)

The veil in the temple was a curtain that blocked the entrance to
the Most Holy Place. Only the High Priest was to enter once a year to
make atonement for himself and the people of God. The tearing of the

veil signifies there is no longer a use for the Leviticus High Priest to make atonement for the children of Israel. The tearing of the veil signifies that God's presence is now open to all though a New Covenant.

The veil tearing from "top to bottom" shows that no person split the veil, but God.

Now, when Jesus died, a new era was born. Jesus' death represents the end of the old covenant. For the new covenant, only one blood sacrifice was needed, Jesus. Now when people come to God, they do not need goats and bulls; they come to God in the name of Jesus Christ. The Levitical priesthood is over. Every person who calls him or herself a child of God is a priest in their own right. The High Priest, Jesus, is now sitting on the right hand of the throne of God. So, as we, as priest, go to our High Priest, Jesus, is to go into the presence of God. "Looking unto Jesus the author and finisher of our faith; who for the joy that was set before him endured the cross, despising the shame, and is set down at the right had of the throne of God" (Hebrews 12:2).

A priest is responsible for building his or her own bridge to reach God. When Jesus died, all of humanity gained the potential to become a priest.

> To whom coming, *as unto* a living stone, disallowed indeed of men, but chosen of God, *and* precious, Ye also, as lively stones, are built up a spiritual house, an holy priesthood, to offer up spiritual sacrifices, acceptable to God by Jesus Christ… But ye *are* a chosen generation, a royal priesthood, an holy nation, a peculiar people; that ye should show forth the praises of him who hath called you out of darkness into his marvellous light. (1 Peter 2:4, 5, 9)

During the Lord's Supper, Jesus offered the disciples the cup of wine and told them to drink. This wine represented the blood of the New Covenant. Also, Jesus' death provided the blood to seal the New Covenant between God and humanity. When the soldiers pierced Jesus in his side at that moment, the New Covenant and new priesthood started.

The first covenant [Mosaic Covenant] is obsolete, "no longer in general use" Hebrews 8:13 says, "In that he saith, A new *covenant*, he hath made the first old. Now that which decayeth and waxeth old *is* ready to vanish away."

In conclusion, a priest is one who is ordained to perform religious rites and make sacrificial offering to a deity. Qualifications of a priest in the New Covenant are repentance, prayer, forgiveness and obedience unto God. Yes, the priesthood still exists. It started when the Israelites (a nation of people) departed from Egypt. Priests minister unto God with praise and worship. The Priesthood is a well-organized group of priests to help the High Priest in carrying out the work of service to God. Jesus Christ is the last, current, and eternal High Priest. He made salvation available for all of humanity. Only you can answer the last question. Are you a priest?

Chapter Seven

The Sinner Woman

Everything in life costs. The price may not be money, but everything has a price tag attached to it. People can be fooled when they do not pay a price at the time of a transaction; however, as life goes on, that payment will come due and the price will be paid. It is like having a credit card; a person can estimate the amount they owe, but the interest will kill you as time goes on. On the other hand, if a person does not save or invest money for their retirement, they may not be able to retire. There is a need to pause and look at this sinner woman's story. What lesson and actions does she need to teach the world? How is the sinner woman's story related to praise and worship? In the story, she pays a price and Jesus gives her something in exchange. It will be unfair to write a book of praise and worship and leave this valuable lesson out. Therefore, here is the sinner woman's story.

> And one of the Pharisees desired him that he would eat with him. And he went into the Pharisee's house, and sat down to meat. And, behold, a woman in the city, which was a sinner, when she knew that *Jesus* sat at meat in the Pharisee's house, brought an alabaster box of ointment, And stood at his feet behind *him* weeping, and began to wash his feet with tears, and did wipe *them* with the hairs of her head, and kissed his feet, and anointed *them* with the ointment. Now when the Pharisee which had bidden him saw *it*, he spake within himself, saying, This man, if he

were a prophet, would have known who and what manner of woman *this is* that toucheth him: for she is a sinner. And Jesus answering said unto him, Simon, I have somewhat to say unto thee. And he saith, Master, say on. There was a certain creditor which had two debtors: the one owed five hundred pence, and the other fifty. And when they had nothing to pay, he frankly forgave them both. Tell me therefore, which of them will love him most? Simon answered and said, I suppose that *he*, to whom he forgave most. And he said unto him, Thou hast rightly judged. And he turned to the woman, and said unto Simon, Seest thou this woman? I entered into thine house, thou gavest me no water for my feet: but she hath washed my feet with tears, and wiped *them* with the hairs of her head. Thou gavest me no kiss: but this woman since the time I came in hath not ceased to kiss my feet. My head with oil thou didst not anoint: but this woman hath anointed my feet with ointment. Wherefore I say unto thee, Her sins, which are many, are forgiven; for she loved much: but to whom little is forgiven, *the same* loveth little. And he said unto her, Thy sins are forgiven. And they that sat at meat with him began to say within themselves, Who is this that forgiveth sins also? And he said to the woman, Thy faith hath saved thee; go in peace. (Luke 7:36-50)

The story began when Jesus was invited for dinner by a Pharisee named Simon in the town of Galilee. He had just healed people of their diseases, cast out evil spirits, and gave sight to the blind. "And the publicans, justified God" they were in agreement with Jesus. They acknowledged that God's way was right. However, the experts in the law and the Pharisees disagreed with Jesus' message (Luke 7:29, 30).

A Pharisee is part of a Jewish sect. They serve God on the outside, making themselves in appearance to be holy and righteous in the eyes of man. But on the inside, their hearts and minds are filthy in the eyes of God. They believe in upholding the tradition (Galatians 1:14) and love to display who they are. They proclaim their position in society by their ancestors, instead of their personal relationship to God.

> Saying, The scribes and the Pharisees sit in Moses' seat….. But all their works they do for to be seen of men: they make broad their phylacteries, and enlarge the borders of their garments, And love the uppermost rooms at feasts, and the chief seats in the synagogues, And greetings in the markets, and to be called of men, Rabbi, Rabbi. (Matthew 23:2, 5-7)

The attitudes of the Pharisees toward Jesus were hostile. They tried to entangle (Matthew 22:15); accuse (Luke 11:53, 54; John 8:3-7); tempt (Matthew 16:1); and destroy (Matthew 12:14) Jesus even to the point of death.

Jesus did not hesitate in accepting the invitation to have dinner with Simon. This demonstrates Jesus' willingness to be available to whoever wants his presence. Now, Jesus' attitude toward the Pharisees was plain throughout the Bible. He referred to them as serpents (Matthew 23:33), hypocrites (Matthew 22:15-22; 23:23), and children of the devil (John 8:44). Son ship is predicated (ground) on conduct. A son will manifest his father's traits. Since some of the Pharisees exhibited the patterns of Satan in their opposition toward Jesus and their failure to believe in Him as Messiah, Jesus deemed them the children of the devil. However, as the story goes, Jesus "went into the Pharisee's house, and sat down to meat" (Luke 7:36).

A Woman in the City

This sinner woman's name does not appear in the scripture. But she was a woman who lived in the city of Galilee. Her sinful nature as a harlot, a woman of the evening, a prostitute is the focus of this story. Her business was selling her most precious asset, her body, for the exchange of money. By the way, she was very prosperous. In the story, this sinner woman did eight things when she encountered Jesus.

First, the sinner woman learned that Jesus was going to have dinner at the Pharisee's house. She took advantage of the opportunity and decided to make her presence known to him. So, she invited herself to the dinner party, into the presence of Jesus. Why did she decide to go to the Pharisee's house? What else could she have heard about Jesus that she sought him out? Talk was in the air. When Jesus was in Nain with his disciples, he raised a widow's son from the dead. The people announced that God's great prophet had "is risen up among us; and, That God hath visited his people. And this rumour of him went forth throughout all Judaea, and throughout all the region round about" (Luke 7:11-17). Also, when Jesus talked about John the Baptist being a messenger of God, "all the people" who heard agreed that God's way was right. She, the sinner woman, could have been in the crowd (Luke 7:24-30). The sinner woman was just like the Pharisee, in that she sought the present of Jesus; however, her motives were different.

Second, the sinner woman brought an alabaster jar of perfume with her. Alabaster is a fine variety of expensive marble, quarried in Egypt, which was carved into delicate containers for storing expensive perfumes. She was educated enough not to come empty handed. Proverbs 3:9 says, "Honour the LORD with thy substance, and with the firstfruits of all thine increase" the word substance means physical matter or material and possessions, means or wealth. The Bible teaches that when one comes into the presence of God, one should bring something to offer Him as a token of love and appreciation.

Third, the sinner woman's position was one of an enemy. She stood behind Jesus at his feet. She knew that she was not worthy to be in His presence. As a custom of the time, Jesus was lounging at a low table. Such dinners involving public figure were often open to viewers. That was how a woman of such low reputation had a chance to approach Jesus at that time. However, to their surprise, the Pharisees did not expect a prostitute to attend. When the sinner woman came to the dinner party, it took great courage, and it shows the extreme concern with which she sought Jesus. Now, as to her position of standing behind Jesus, this is the place for the enemy; it belongs to those who oppose the will of God. For example, when the children of Israel departed for Egypt, the army was behind them and drowned in the sea (Exodus 14:19-28). When Satan himself was tempting Jesus, Jesus told Satan, "Get thee behind me, Satan: for it is written, Thou shalt worship the Lord thy God, and him only shalt thou serve" (Luke 4:8); because Jesus knew the position of the enemy should be behind a child of God. The full armor of God (Ephesians 6:11-18) has no protection for the back, because God has the back of all saints. Therefore, when the enemy is trying to attack a saint from the back, that battle is directly dealt with by God. One can only imagine how this sinner woman felt coming into an uninvited dinner party, with a gift in her hands, in the position of an enemy. Most of all, she realized and acknowledge her position in God.

Fourth, the sinner woman wept while she was at the feet of Jesus. Weeping is when someone is crying and tears are shed. Weeping is an outward sign of an inner transformation. This woman weeping was an expression of deep repentance. She was sorry for her past behaviors. She was changing. Tears also are a sign of sorrow. She was sorry for the sins that she had committed that had separated her from the fellowship of God. Psalm 34:18 says, "The LORD *is* nigh unto them that are of a broken heart; and saveth such as be of a contrite spirit." Brokenness is like taking a reflection in a mirror that represents a person's character, actions and attitudes, throwing it to the ground because it does not please God, and allowing God to put the mirror back together in the way that seems good to Him.

Fifth and sixth go together; the sinner woman was washing Jesus' feet with her tears and wiping them with her hair. In the days when Jesus walked the earth, washing a guest's feet was an essential custom. Simon, the Pharisee, had invited Jesus and did not offer him any water to wash his feet, which was a total insult to his guest. Nevertheless, in the sinner woman's brokenness, her tears wet Jesus feet, so she took the opportunity to wipe them. Washing is done to loosen dirt and grime out of a fabric. Her tears were employing, confessing, or acknowledging her dirt and grime (sins) to Jesus. Nobody offered her a towel, so she bowed down (Barak) and used her hair. Psalm 95:6 say, "O come, let us worship and bow down: let us kneel before the LORD our maker." Now that Jesus bore her sins, she could come into a position to worship God. The sinner woman's hair became her towel. As she wiped His feet, it represented the removed the dirt completely. That is what salvation is, a complete forgiveness of sin in Jesus Christ our Lord. Her hair is her glory. "But if a woman have long hair, it is a glory to her" (1 Corinthians 11:15). Jesus, she said with her actions, I bow down to the lowest part of your existence, your feet, and wipe them with my glory, my hair, in the presence of those who hate me. This woman's actions showed those dining with Jesus how salvation looks. Today she is teaching us. Her action was saying, my glory is no comparison to your feet. To bow down is to give up your position, your way of thinking and doing things, and to submit to the will of God.

Seventh, the sinner woman kissed Jesus' feet continually. A kiss is a sign of love and tender affection toward someone. The sinner woman was not looking for a one night stand. She was seeking for a lifelong, loving, and righteous relationship. Earnest repentance and broken heartedness is critical to an everlasting, godly relationship. In Matthew 22:34-40, the Pharisees were testing Jesus when one of them asks him "*a question*, tempting him, and saying, Master, which *is* the great commandment in the law? Jesus said unto him, Thou shalt love the Lord thy God with all thy heart, and with all thy soul, and with all thy mind." God is looking for someone to love Him by their words and actions. The sinner woman demonstrated unconditional love toward Jesus in the midst of her situation.

Eighth, the sinner woman anointed Jesus' feet with the expensive fragrant oil that she brought with her to the dinner party. To anoint is "to rub or sprinkle on, to smear with any liquid, to move something back and forth or with a rotary motion as against or along another surface." Anointing

Jesus' feet with the expensive fragrant oil allowed the sinner woman and Jesus to smell the same. As she moved her hands back and forth, the fragrance penetrated the skin of her hands and the skin of Jesus' feet. They both smelled alike. Jesus allows humanity to make connections with Him in spite of their past reputation and sins.

The Pharisee and the Sinner Woman

Throughout the story, the Pharisee and the sinner woman have traits that are similar and different. First, they both are sinners and have a need for salvation. "For all have sinned, and come short of the glory of God" (Romans 3:23). Jesus has indicated in His story to Simon that whether a debt (sin) is a little or a lot, humanity is unable to pay it. Humanity has a need for God's intervention of forgiveness of sin through Jesus the Christ. Second, both the Pharisee and the sinner woman did not say a spoken word; however, Simon only answers to Jesus' question. In this story, Jesus was dealing with their inner man—the real essence of the person. Third, they both had access to Jesus.

The differences between the Pharisee and the sinner woman are many. First, the Pharisee has invited Jesus into his house; the sinner woman invited Jesus into her heart. Second, the Pharisee did not respect Jesus by not providing water to wash, and a towel to dry his feet or oil to anoint his head. The sinner woman gave Jesus high respect by using her tears to wash, her hair to wipe, and expensive oil to anoint His feet. Third, the Pharisee sat at the table with Jesus at eye level. This is the position of a colleague or a friend. But the sinner woman prostrated herself at Jesus' feet; she bowed down her will, attitude, and desires to Jesus' authority. Fourth, the Pharisee did not kiss Jesus' face as he stood in front of Him. But the sinner woman over and over again kissed Jesus' feet. Fifth, the Pharisee had thoughts of evil about the sinner woman. Because of the sinner woman's character, Simon thought that Jesus would send her away, because for her touching Him was supposed to pass on ceremonial uncleanness. The Bible does not say anything about the sinner woman's

Doris J Sanders

thoughts. Sixth, the Pharisee had no faith in Jesus; his thoughts clearly articulate his suspicions, "This man, if he were a prophet" (Luke 7:39). Jesus knew and answered Simon's thoughts, an act that clearly indicated that He was indeed a prophet. Seventh, the sinner woman had faith in Jesus being sent from God and received forgiveness and salvation, a changed life. "Thy faith hath saved thee" (Luke 7:50). The Pharisee did not receive forgiveness for his sins; no change occurred. Despite all of the acts of love the sinner woman displayed toward Jesus, including the sorrow in her heart move her into the area of salvation, but her faith brought about a change. "If we confess our sins, he is faithful and just to forgive us *our* sins, and to cleanse us from all unrighteousness" (1 John 1:9).

Day of Atonement—Ministry of Reconciliation

The sinner woman experience is a type of atonement or an illustration of what the new covenant calls the ministry of reconciliation. There is very significant meaning for all of the events that take place on the Day of Atonement. The Day of Atonement was the most important of the regulations given to Israel because on that day, atonement was made for all the sins of the high priest and the entire congregation. This is the only ordinance that required the congregation to fast, to deny themselves of physical pleasures. The High Priest went into the Holy of Holies once a year to perform the ritual for forgiveness of sins for himself and Israel. The blood that was shed was from a goat that was set aside for that purpose for the sins of all the people. Afterward the second goat, the scapegoat, was left alive to carry away the sins of Israel. This scapegoat was led and left in the wilderness.

> And he shall take of the congregation of the children of Israel two kids of the goats for a sin offering, and one ram for a burnt offering. And Aaron shall offer his bullock of the sin offering, which *is* for himself, and make an atonement for himself, and for his house. And he shall take the two

goats, and present them before the LORD *at* the door of the tabernacle of the congregation. And Aaron shall cast lots upon the two goats; one lot for the LORD, and the other lot for the scapegoat. And Aaron shall bring the goat upon which the LORD'S lot fell, and offer him *for* a sin offering. But the goat, on which the lot fell to be the scapegoat, shall be presented alive before the LORD, to make an atonement with him, *and* to let him go for a scapegoat into the wilderness.

And he shall take of the blood of the bullock, and sprinkle *it* with his finger upon the mercy seat eastward; and before the mercy seat shall he sprinkle of the blood with his finger seven times. Then shall he kill the goat of the sin offering, that *is* for the people, and bring his blood within the veil, and do with that blood as he did with the blood of the bullock, and sprinkle it upon the mercy seat, and before the mercy seat: And he shall make an atonement for the holy *place*, because of the uncleanness of the children of Israel, and because of their transgressions in all their sins: and so shall he do for the tabernacle of the congregation, that remaineth among them in the midst of their uncleanness. And there shall be no man in the tabernacle of the congregation when he goeth in to make an atonement in the holy *place*, until he come out, and have made an atonement for himself, and for his household, and for all the congregation of Israel.

And when he hath made an end of reconciling the holy *place*, and the tabernacle of the congregation, and the altar, he shall bring the live goat: And Aaron shall lay both his hands upon the head of the live goat, and confess over him all the iniquities of the children of Israel, and all their transgressions in all their sins, putting them upon the head of the goat, and shall send *him* away by the hand of a fit man into the wilderness: And the goat shall bear upon him all their iniquities unto a land not inhabited: and he shall let go the goat in the wilderness.

And he shall wash his flesh with water in the holy place, and put on his garments, and come forth, and offer his burnt offering, and the burnt offering of the people, and make an atonement for himself, and for the people. And the fat of the sin offering shall he burn upon the altar.

And *this* shall be a statute for ever unto you: *that* in the seventh month, on the tenth *day* of the month, ye shall afflict your souls, and do no work at all, *whether it be* one of your own country, or a stranger that sojourneth among you: For on that day shall *the priest* make an atonement for you, to cleanse you, *that* ye may be clean from all your sins before the LORD.

And this shall be an everlasting statute unto you, to make an atonement for the children of Israel for all their sins once a year. And he did as the LORD commanded Moses. (Leviticus 16:5-10, 14-17, 20-22, 24-25, 29-30, 34)

The Day of Atonement shows how the sins of Israel are removed and placed back to the source of sin, the Devil. It is a shadow of the New Covenant fulfillment: Ministry of Reconciliation. The first male goat used as a sin offering is Jesus. Only his blood is qualified to remove the sins of humanity. The blood of the goat was sprinkle seven times before the atonement cover behind the curtain. The number seven represents completion. Therefore, the sins of Israel are completely forgiven by the blood. While the high priest—Aaron at this time—was performing the atonement, nobody was allowed in the Tent of Meeting until he came out. After the children of Israel's sins were completely forgiven, Aaron proceeds with the scapegoat. This goat was kept alive and took on the sins of Israel by Aaron laying both of his hands on its head. An appointed man led the scapegoat to a solitary place.

In the New Covenant, Jesus is the Lamb of God. He had to enter into the holy place once for the sins of all of humanity. His sacrifice is permanent with no need to be repeated. As of now, Jesus is still in the Most Holy Place making atonement for new believers confessing their sins and asking for forgiveness. "Looking unto Jesus the author and finisher of *our* faith; who for the joy that was set before him endured the cross, despising the shame, and is set down at the right hand of the throne of God" (Hebrews 12:2). However, that does not mean that a person should sin after they have knowledge and understanding of right and wrong. The Bible warns believers of the judgment of intention (plan) act of sin. "For if we sin wilfully after that we have received the knowledge of the truth, there remaineth no more sacrifice for sins, But a certain fearful looking for of judgment and fiery indignation, which shall devour the adversaries" (Hebrews 10:26, 27). The sinner woman's story shows how reconciliation happens.

> Therefore if any man *be* in Christ, *he is* a new creature: old things are passed away; behold, all things are become new. And all things *are* of God, who hath reconciled us to himself by Jesus Christ, and hath given to us the ministry of reconciliation; To wit, that God was in Christ, reconciling the world unto himself, not imputing their trespasses unto them; and hath committed unto us the word of reconciliation. Now then we are ambassadors for Christ, as though God did beseech *you* by us: we pray *you* in Christ's stead, be ye reconciled to God. For he hath made him *to be* sin for us, who knew no sin; that we might be made the righteousness of God in him. (2 Corinthians 5:17-21)

Reconciliation is between God and sinners through Jesus Christ. It involves a changed relationship from one of enemies to family. All the aspects related to someone's conversion and newly transformed lives in Christ are proficiently managed by God. God has called all believers to accept the opportunity of serving unbelievers by proclaiming (publicizing) the gospel (good new) of reconciliation to others.

Leviticus 16:20-22 this second goat represents the old dragon, the Devil. He was the one in the Garden of Eden that deceived Adam and Eve and all humanity into a sinful life, one of rebellion to God. He will take on the punishment due him for his deeds. The one appointed will cast him away into an Abyss. The word abyss means "a deep immeasurable space, gulf or cavity."

> And I saw an angel come down from heaven, having the key of the bottomless pit and a great chain in his hand. And he laid hold on the dragon, that old serpent, which is the Devil, and Satan, and bound him a thousand years, And cast him into the bottomless pit, and shut him up, and set a seal upon him, that he should deceive the nations no more, till the thousand years should be fulfilled: and after that he must be loosed a little season. (Revelation 20:1-3)

When the scapegoat is released into the wilderness, solitary, or abyss, the high priest is to offer a burnt offering. This burnt offering is one of fellowship (peace) between God and humanity; this fire must not go out (Leviticus 6:8-13). Like the apostle Paul said, "Pray without ceasing" (1 Thessalonians 5:17). Communicating with God through prayer keeps the peace and fellowship between God and yourself, which is the essence of man. Solomon, the wisest man who ever lived, stated, "Let us hear the conclusion of the whole matter: Fear God, and keep his commandments: for this *is* the whole *duty* of man" (Ecclesiastes 12:13). Listed below are the differences between the Day of Atonement and the Ministry of Reconciliation.

Day of Atonement	Ministry of Reconciliation
Old Covenant	New Covenant
High Priest—manHigh (the tribe of Levite)	Priest—Jesus (God) (the tribe of Judah)
Animal sacrifice erroneous	Jesus is sacrifice perfect
Yearly ceremony (Israel forgiven once a year)	One time event (Jesus sacrifice once, but humanity daily forgiveness)
Israel sins—twelve tribes	World sins—all humanity
Temporary forgiveness (Incomplete)	Permanent forgiveness (Complete, conscious)
Forgiveness through High Priest to God	Forgiveness through Jesus to God
Forgiveness through physical acts	Forgiveness through faith

The Other Guests

The Bible did not say who the other guests were. They observe the behavior of Simon and the sinner woman. Simon treated Jesus with disrespect. The sinner woman approached Jesus as an enemy and gave Him all the best that she had, even her heart. The other guests heard the story that Jesus told Simon and witnessed to his response. When Jesus declared that he had forgiven the sinner woman of her sins, the other guests were shocked and troubled. By their response, they did not believe in Jesus as well. They tipped their hand when they said among themselves, "Who is this that forgiveth sins also?" (Luke 7:49). At that moment, they realized that they did not know who they were dining with and the power God has entrusted with Jesus as the Lamb of God.

In conclusion, as we come into the presence of God, we are the alabaster flask, the most precious thing that God has made in the universe. What is inside of our alabaster flask is praise and worship, the most expensive commodity in the universe. Nevertheless, no matter how wonderful or glorious one's praise is toward God, be it physical or vocal, one must have faith in God to receive salvation. So the sinner woman's story has taught the world that acts of love toward God cannot take the place of faith.

> That if thou shalt confess with thy mouth the Lord Jesus, and shalt believe in thine heart that God hath raised him from the dead, thou shalt be saved. For with the heart man believeth unto righteousness; and with the mouth confession is made unto salvation. (Romans 10:9, 10)

> But without faith *it is* impossible to please *him*: for he that cometh to God must believe that he is, and *that* he is a rewarder of them that diligently seek him. (Hebrews 11:6)

Chapter Eight

Praise and Kingdom Work

When the children of God gather in the house of the Lord, it is not just that they can feel the power of the Lord like a drug that gives the body the feeling of euphoria. God has some goals in this praise experience of His own. First, when people praise and worship God, it allows the world to know about His goodness and mercy. Praise and worship is a life style, not just a two hour event on Sunday morning. It is how one thinks, talks, lives, and carries oneself from moment to moment. Second, God wants all of humanity to learn how to have life more abundantly and to seek an opportunity to become His sons and daughters. Third, God has assigned works and spiritual gifts for His people so they can be productive. Children of God are His ambassadors (2 Corinthians 5:20). As His ambassadors, one is to do God's work here on earth. A church is like a spiritual school, a school which teaches people the word of God to empower them in this walk of life. Fourth, the conduct for membership and kingdomship is very important. The power of God is needed at times to help, to stay, or establish a conduct acceptable to Him. After all, who would want to go through the Christian experience and give their time, labor, and money to have it all counted in vain? The word vain means worthless, without success or results. Jesus taught a sermon on the mountainside. It was about people who claimed they did the work of God, but Jesus' reply was one of denial and rejection.

> Not every one that saith unto me, Lord, Lord, shall enter
> into the kingdom of heaven; but he that doeth the will of

my Father which is in heaven. Many will say to me in that day, Lord, Lord, have we not prophesied in thy name? and in thy name have cast out devils? and in thy name done many wonderful works? And then will I profess unto them, I never knew you: depart from me, ye that work iniquity. Therefore whosoever heareth these sayings of mine, and doeth them, I will liken him unto a wise man, which built his house upon a rock. (Matthew 7:21-24)

Striving for the kingdom of God is what life is all about. King Solomon, the richest and wisest man who ever lived, put the saying like this, "Let us hear the conclusion of the whole matter: Fear God, and keep his commandments: for this *is* the whole *duty* of man" (Ecclesiastes 12:13). This chapter reveals how God operates during praise and worship in one's life. Praise and worship are a way of life in conduct and deed, not just in words.

God Displays His Goodness and Mercy

Praise and worship are not one-sided. There is a giver (you) and a receiver (God). God wants the world to know of His goodness and mercy. Praise and worship are a benefit of recognition that God receives from delivering one out of a dilemma. It gives credit to the deity who takes action on man's behalf. Sometimes people do not get what they want from God, answers to their problems, deliverance, healing, etc. because God knows He will not get what He wants: praise (credit). Satan's goal is to kill, steal, and destroy all of humanity and to put them in bondage. God wants humanity to be free and prosperous (John 10:10; Joshua 1:8, 9). The Bible has several great events showing God's goodness and mercy. The story about King Nebuchadnezzar and the three Hebrew men is great. Their lifestyle demonstrated true praise and worship unto the death. Their trust in God made them live a steadfast life of obedience, which granted them earthly kingdom protection, and prosperity.

The story begins with three Hebrew men that would not bow down to the idol gods of the king. They have made a premeditated decision not to bow down to the king's gods. They had a God of their own to obey. God told these three Hebrew men to obey, praise and bow down only to Him.

> Thou shalt have no other gods before me. Thou shalt not make unto thee any graven image, or any likeness *of any thing* that *is* in heaven above, or that *is* in the earth beneath, or that *is* in the water under the earth: Thou shalt not bow down thyself to them, nor serve them: for I the LORD thy God *am* a jealous God, visiting the iniquity of the fathers upon the children unto the third and fourth *generation* of them that hate me. (Exodus 20:3-5)

However, they were in physical bondage but they were spiritually free (Daniel 1:1-7; 3:12). Here is the story.

> Nebuchadnezzar the king made an image of gold, whose height *was* threescore cubits, *and* the breadth thereof six cubits: he set it up in the plain of Dura, in the province of Babylon. Then Nebuchadnezzar the king sent to gather together the princes, the governors, and the captains, the judges, the treasurers, the counsellors, the sheriffs, and all the rulers of the provinces, to come to the dedication of the image which Nebuchadnezzar the king had set up.

> Then an herald cried aloud, To you it is commanded, O people, nations, and languages, *That* at what time ye hear the sound of the cornet, flute, harp, sackbut, psaltery, dulcimer, and all kinds of music, ye fall down and worship the golden image that Nebuchadnezzar the king hath set up: And whoso falleth not down and worshippeth shall the same hour be cast into the midst of a burning fiery furnace.

Wherefore at that time certain Chaldeans came near, and accused the Jews.

There are certain Jews whom thou hast set over the affairs of the province of Babylon, Shadrach, Meshach, and Abednego; these men, O king, have not regarded thee: they serve not thy gods, nor worship the golden image which thou hast set up. Then Nebuchadnezzar in *his* rage and fury commanded to bring Shadrach, Meshach, and Abednego. Then they brought these men before the king. Nebuchadnezzar spake and said unto them, *Is it* true, O Shadrach, Meshach, and Abednego, do not ye serve my gods, nor worship the golden image which I have set up? Now if ye be ready that at what time ye hear the sound of the cornet, flute, harp, sackbut, psaltery, and dulcimer, and all kinds of music, ye fall down and worship the image which I have made; *well*: but if ye worship not, ye shall be cast the same hour into the midst of a burning fiery furnace; and who *is* that God that shall deliver you out of my hands? Shadrach, Meshach, and Abednego, answered and said to the king, O Nebuchadnezzar, we *are* not careful to answer thee in this matter. If it be *so*, our God whom we serve is able to deliver us from the burning fiery furnace, and he will deliver *us* out of thine hand, O king. But if not, be it known unto thee, O king, that we will not serve thy gods, nor worship the golden image which thou hast set up....*therefore* he spake, and commanded that they should heat the furnace one seven times more than it was wont to be heated.

And these three men, Shadrach, Meshach, and Abednego, fell down bound into the midst of the burning fiery furnace.

Then Nebuchadnezzar came near to the mouth of the burning fiery furnace, *and* spake, and said, Shadrach, Meshach, and Abednego, ye servants of the most high God, come forth, and come *hither*. Then Shadrach, Meshach, and Abednego, came forth of the midst of the fire. And the princes, governors, and captains, and the king's counsellors, being gathered together, saw these men, upon whose bodies the fire had no power, nor was an hair of their head singed, neither were their coats changed, nor the smell of fire had passed on them. *Then* Nebuchadnezzar spake, and said, Blessed *be* the God of Shadrach, Meshach, and Abednego, who hath sent his angel, and delivered his servants that trusted in him, and have changed the king's word, and yielded their bodies, that they might not serve nor worship any god, except their own God. Therefore I make a decree, That every people, nation, and language, which speak any thing amiss against the God of Shadrach, Meshach, and Abednego, shall be cut in pieces, and their houses shall be made a dunghill: because there is no other God that can deliver after this sort. Then the king promoted Shadrach, Meshach, and Abednego, in the province of Babylon. (Daniel 3:1-2, 4-6, 8, 12-18, 19b, 23, 26-30)

The obedience of these three men, Shadrach, Meshach and Abednego, to God allowed Him to display His goodness and mercy. This event had national attention. The whole kingdom was watching, the high officials crowded around these men after coming out of the furnace. These men worshiped God with their mouth and actions to the point of death. Even the king declared that, "there is no other God that can deliver after this sort" (v.29). Walking after God is not an easy task, but the Bible say, "and, lo, I am with you alway, *even* unto the end of the world" (Matthew 28:20). Shadrach, Meshach and Abednego, knew that this battle, struggle, and conflict belong to God. That is why they said, "we do not need to defend ourselves before you in this matter" (v.16 NIV). The people of Judah had this problem before in the past when King Jehoshaphat reigned (2 Chronicles 20). This story had to be told to these men; they were accustomed to being taught the history of their people.

There were two blessings given to Shadrach, Meshach and Abednego for their faith and loyalty in God, beside their life. First, the king gave them physical protection. The king had decreed, "Therefore I [King Nebuchadnezzar] make a decree, That every people, nation, and language, which speak any thing amiss against the God of Shadrach, Meshach, and Abednego, shall be cut in pieces, and their houses shall be made a dunghill" (v.29a). Second, they received a promotion by the king on their jobs. Promotion means more power, prestige and money.

Salvation and Prosperity

God has a desire that all humanity will be saved and prosper. Jesus was talking to his disciples about spreading the good news of salvation to everyone. God wants all men, women, boys and girls to come into the knowledge of His plans of salvation to all who believe. All the lines of race, color, creed, sex and age were erased.

> Go ye therefore, and teach all nations, baptizing them in
> the name of the Father, and of the Son, and of the Holy
> Ghost: Teaching them to observe all things whatsoever
> I have commanded you: and, lo, I am with you alway,
> *even* unto the end of the world. Amen. (Matthew 28:19,
> 20)

The qualifications to be a disciple are easy. First, believe that God exists; second, obey His every word. Obedience to God is not like a salad bar, to pick and choose what you want to obey. Jesus explains it in John 8:30, 31; it says, "As he spake these words, many believed on him. Then said Jesus to those Jews which believed on him, If ye continue in my word, *then* are ye my disciples indeed." The word "abides" means, to dwell, to remain, to stay. Therefore, a disciple is one who believes and obeys God and maintains their loyalty to the whole truth of God. God wants humanity to live a life of more abundance: more peace, more love, more health, and more prosperity. Jesus makes it plain in John 10:10. The laws of God direct one on how to receive a prosperous life if the laws are applied. In other words, obedience to God's word is prosperity (Joshua 1:7, 8), the secret to true and lasting prosperity.

> Only be thou strong and very courageous, that thou mayest observe to do according to all the law, which Moses my servant commanded thee: turn not from it *to* the right hand or *to* the left, that thou mayest prosper whithersoever thou goest. 8 This book of the law shall not depart out of thy mouth; but thou shalt meditate therein day and night, that thou mayest observe to do according to all that is written therein: for then thou shalt make thy way prosperous, and then thou shalt have good success.

Even the apostle John understood this concept that God wants his people to prosper. John spoke of this blessing of prosperity in his last letter he wrote. "Beloved, I wish above all things that thou mayest prosper and be in health, even as thy soul prospereth" (3 John 2). How can a soul prosper? The word soul in this verse means, "The spiritual part of humans regarded in its moral aspect, thought and action in humans." There is a direct relationship between spiritual growth and physical blessing. The more a person uses the instruction book (Holy Bible) and principles of God, the more they prosper. In order to use the principles, one must learn and study them, meditate on them, and keep them close at hand.

Doris J Sanders

Spiritual Work: Ambassador of God

There is a story, a true event, about a young colt. This colt represents anyone, or should I say everyone, who is an ambassador of God. An ambassador is "an official envoy: a diplomatic agent of the highest rank accredited to a foreign government or sovereign as the resident representative of his or her own government or sovereign or appointment for a special and often temporary diplomatic assignment." A Christian's assignment is to help humanity to become reconciled to God directly and indirectly. A direct ambassador is one who teaches the ways of God to whoever is willing to learn. An indirect ambassador is one who lives the ways of God for all to see and observe. All true ambassadors are both. This story of a young colt shows how God works in one's life to obtain freedom and then works to help others obtain theirs.

> And it came to pass, when He drew near to Bethphage and Bethany, at the mountain call Olivet, that He sent two of His disciples, saying, "Go into the village opposite you, where as you enter you will find a colt tied, on which no one has ever sat. Loose it and bring it here. And if anyone asks you, 'Why are you loosing it?' thus you shall say to him, 'Because the Lord has need of it.'" So those who were sent went their way and found it just as He had said to them. But as they were loosing the colt, the owners of it said to them, "Why are you loosing the colt?" And they said, "The Lord has need of him." Then they brought him to Jesus. And they threw their own clothes on the colt, and they set Jesus on him. And as He went, many spread their clothes on the road. Then, as He was now drawing near the descent of the Mount of Olives, the whole multitude of the disciples began to rejoice and praise God with a loud voice for all the mighty works they had seen, saying: "'Blessed is the King who comes in the name of the Lord!'

Peace in heaven and glory in the highest! "And some of the Pharisees called to Him from the crowd, "Teacher, rebuke Your disciples." But He answered and said to them, "I tell you that if these should keep silent, the stones would immediately cry out." (Luke 19:29-40 NKJV)

I would like to point out ten things about this colt. First, this colt was young and inexperienced. Second, Jesus knew the location of the colt. He had given the disciples the precise direction, location, and situation of the colt. Third, Jesus knew the events that had and had not occurred in the colt's life. The colt was tied and no one had ever sat on his back. Fourth, Jesus knew that the colt could not loose himself. Jesus told his two disciples to loose the colt and bring him to Himself. Fifth, Jesus knew that the owner was going to ask about his colt being loose. Jesus gave his ambassadors a response to give the owner before they left on their journey. Sixth, they allowed the colt into the present of Jesus. Seventh, the colt was tamed immediately by Jesus. Eight, the colt took Jesus where He needed to go. Ninth, they laid out the colt's path before him. Tenth, the position of the colt was one of being bowed down [Barak], so that Jesus could ride him.

Now, let us compare the colt to humanity in the ten points discussed earlier. First, we are or were young and inexperienced Christians. As babies in Christ, we were first fed with milk. "As newborn babes, desire the sincere milk of the word, that ye may grow thereby: If so be ye have tasted that the Lord *is* gracious" (1 Peter 2:2, 3). However, being babies in Christ is only the beginning. As time goes on, a Christian should develop into full maturity, being able to understand and live on solid Spiritual food (1 Corinthians 3:1, 2; Hebrews 5:12-14). Second, Jesus knows our physical location and our state of minds. In Luke 19:30, Jesus told His disciples to go to the village opposite of themselves. The word opposite means sharply contrasting, away from each other, to be in conflict, to be in disagreement with. In order for the disciples to get the colt, the location they traveled in was opposite where they were going. Now, there are only two sides to everything: right or wrong, good or bad, Godly or Satanic, heaven or hell. There- fore, the colt was on the wrong side, the bad side, the satanic side, and the bound for the hell side. So, when God came looking for us, we were on the wrong side, the bad side, the satanic side, and the bound for the hell side (Romans 7:12-20). Third, Jesus knows the events that have occurred in one's life (Romans 3:23). He knows the past, present, and future. Jesus knows to what and who we are in bondage. In Ephesians 1:3-10, Jesus said he saved us from the foundation of the world. There are events and destinies attach to our lives that have not unfold yet, but, it is predestined. When the expected time comes, it will unfold itself. Fourth, Jesus sent two disciples to loose the colt. Now, Jesus knows that humanity cannot loose themselves. He has given two things to loosen humanity. First, He given His Word, "And ye shall know the truth, and the truth shall make you free" (John 8:32). The second thing is the Holy Spirit. 2 Corinthians 3:17, states that, "Now the Lord is that Spirit: and where the Spirit of the Lord *is*, there *is* liberty." After one is set free from bondage, they can present themselves to God as available vessels. Fifth, Jesus knew that the owner of the colt was going to question the release of his property. Satan, who has humanity fastened and locked up, will also put up noise when freedom comes to his captives. But, take a closer look at what happened. The disciples said, **"Because the Lord hath need of him"** (Luke 19:31). When the Word, Jesus, is manifest, Satan, or that thing that has one in bondage, is tame and subjected to the authority of God. The owner never said another word, but is under direct order to release the one that is being held captive (Philippians 2:9, 10). Sixth, the colt was permitted into the presence of Jesus. The disciples had prepared the colt before they put Jesus on his back. People cannot just walk into the presence of God. The two disciples threw their own garments on the colt; this is a time of preparing the colt for the work of God. The colt had to be educated for his purpose. Repentance, praying and praise are some instruments used by believers to prepare for an audience before the King. God tells his children to come boldly into his presence. "Let us therefore come boldly unto the throne of grace, that we may obtain mercy, and find grace to help in time of need" (Hebrews 4:16). This is the time you should humble yourself to the will of God. At this moment, Spiritual growth is occurring. Seventh, the colt was tamed immediately by Jesus. As soon as Jesus was on the colt's back, the connection happened. The colt never cast or fought to get rid of Jesus. There was a sense of peace, harmony and cooperation that occurred—atonement (Amos 3:3). We are to be obedient immediately in the presence of God. When we know that God wants something, we should do it straightway with a sense of submission, joy, and love. The Lord has need of us. Eighth, the colt took Jesus where He needed to go. We are to take Jesus where He needs to go: home, work, school, family reunions, restaurants, mall, movies, etc. (Matthew 5:14-16). Ninth, the colt's path was pointed out before him as he traveled on his way. This is how children of God are led, as we travel on our daily journey, the Word of God guides our every step. Some examples are: love your enemies, do not judge, do not worry, and do not bear false witness. Whatever situation that comes up in one's life, the Bible has an answer for everything. Tenth, the position of the colt was one of being bowed down [Barak] so that Jesus could ride him. This is how we are lifting Jesus up. One must develop and maintain an attitude of humility. We are giving honor and glory unto God when we take Him into other people's lives, directly or indirectly.

Sunday after Sunday, month after month, we always hear the saints saying, "We really had **church**!" Some people would say that, "the Spirit of God dwells in the church during praise and worship services!" Some people will say they shouted their trouble out or over. Other people were speaking in tongues; some were getting delivered by the laying on of hands. The praise team leader would say, "Who came to have **church** today!" The Children of Israel, who taught us how to praise God, also had a dilemma about having "**church.**" These activities during services are good; this is what God wants for his children, deliverance, healing, and rejoicing, but the buck does not stop there. We must go a little farther in this conversation. The prophet Amos has a message to give all about having "**church!**" In this passage, God was talking about his people's actions as they came into the temple to praise him.

> I hate, I despise your feast days, and I will not smell in your solemn assemblies. Though ye offer me burnt offerings and your meat offerings, I will not accept *them*: neither will I regard the peace offerings of your fat beasts. Take thou away from me the noise of thy songs; for I will not hear the melody of thy viols [stringed instruments]. (Amos 5:21-23)

This is a major problem. How strange this is! The God of all creation hates the very things that His has set into motion. This is not the first time God told His people to shut up. The prophet Isaiah records an incident about worship that displeased God earlier.

> To what purpose *is* the multitude of your sacrifices unto me? saith the LORD: I am full of the burnt offerings of rams, and the fat of fed beasts; and I delight not in the blood of bullocks, or of lambs, or of he goats. When ye come to appear before me, who hath required this at your hand, to tread my courts? Bring no more vain oblations; incense is an abomination unto me; the new moons and sabbaths, the calling of assemblies, I cannot away with; *it is* iniquity, even the solemn meeting. Your new moons and your appointed feasts my soul hateth: they are a trouble unto me; I am weary to bear *them*. And when ye spread forth your hands, I will hide mine eyes from you: yea, when ye make many prayers, I will not hear: your hands are full of blood. (Isaiah 1:11-15)

God was not delighted in their praise experience, because sin was present among the members in the temple. He was tired of them seeking their own selfish ambitions. God was tired of them doing a new thing and never having any new or increased Godly behavior. A lot of audio tapes, CDs, DVDs, and conferences are a carbon copy of the same. Why do people need to be revitalized, when they were, already vitalized but did not do anything with that vitalization? When God sees that the results of good **church** is more good **church**, and not work, God says, I am out of here. The end result of praise and worship should be work. Any worship that God rejects is because the worshiper is only caring for himself or herself. Who is hindering one from doing the work of God? Who is stopping one from receiving their miracles? The only person that can hold one back is you.

God even hated their fast.

> Wherefore have we fasted, *say they*, and thou seest not? *wherefore* have we afflicted our soul, and thou takest no knowledge? Behold, in the day of your fast ye find pleasure, and exact all your labours. Behold, ye fast for strife and debate, and to smite with the fist of wickedness: ye shall not fast as *ye do this* day, to make your voice to be heard on high. Is it such a fast that I have chosen? a day for a man to afflict his soul? *is it* to bow down his head as a bulrush, and to spread sackcloth and ashes *under him*? wilt thou call this a fast, and an acceptable day to the LORD? (Isaiah 58:3-5)

Why did God hate and reject their worship and fast? He is the one who taught them how to worship and fast. God rejected their worship and fast because they made an idol out of worshiping and fasting. People should not worship just because it feels good or fast so that they can lose some weight or start a body cleanings program. Worship and fasting is like taking a bath; it gets one prepared to bring forth an event, Godly work. What events should worship bring forth? The Bible has listed eight things that worship should produce.

> But let judgment run down as waters, and righteousness as a mighty stream. (Amos 5:24)

> Wash you, make you clean; put away the evil of your doings from before mine eyes; cease to do evil; Learn to do well; seek judgment, relieve the oppressed, judge the fatherless, plead for the widow. (Isaiah 1:16, 17)

Fasting is a spiritual tool that God has implemented to help His people to accomplish their goals. It has seven spiritual functions. Fasting help one to be sensitive to other's needs. Fasting can help to place a person in a proper and direct relationship with God.

> *Is* not this the fast that I have chosen? to loose the bands of wickedness, to undo the heavy burdens, and to let the oppressed go free, and that ye break every yoke? *Is it* not to deal thy bread to the hungry, and that thou bring the poor that are cast out to thy house? when thou seest the naked, that thou cover him; and that thou hide not thyself from thine own flesh? Then shall thy light break forth as the morning, and thine health shall spring forth speedily: and thy righteousness shall go before thee; the glory of the LORD shall be thy rereward. Then shalt thou call, and the LORD shall answer; thou shalt cry, and he shall say, Here I *am*. If thou take away from the midst of thee the yoke, the putting forth of the finger, and speaking vanity. (Isaiah 58:6-9)

Now we know that going to **church** is more than just receiving a good feeling. Worship and fasting are the beginning process of doing the work of God and should be taken very seriously. It is ok to enjoy the worship experience, but do not forget the larger picture. The end result of praise, worship, and fasting is spiritual work.

Membership, Kingdomship and Spiritual Conduct

What is membership? What is kingdomship? Moreover, what do membership and kingdomship have to do with praise and worship? Membership is
"the state of being a member, as of a society, club" or church. Kingdomship
is being a member in the kingdom of God under the rule of the king, in this
case, Jesus. Church membership is the physical, temporary state that
humanity is in now. Some rules, regulations and traditions are created
by the church organizations. The church requires that church members
abide by these rules, regulations, and traditions that the organization has
set in motion in order to keep their membership status. Kingdomship is
spiritual and everlasting in nature. The rules and regulations are set by
God. Kingdomship is the goal for all believers in Jesus for now and the
future.

Now, praise and worship is what is happening in heaven today (Isaiah
6:1-4). When Jesus taught us how to pray, it included God's kingdom
coming and his will be done, "After this manner therefore pray ye: Our
Father which art in heaven, Hallowed be thy name. Thy kingdom come.
Thy will be done in earth, as *it is* in heaven" (Matthew 6:9, 10). All the
saints of God want to be a part of that heavenly worship and praise
service. Kingdom work, operating in one's spiritual gifts, is good and
necessary, but obedience to God is key, to be in the Kingdom now and
tomorrow. A person's every day conduct is very important for being in the
Kingdom of God. "We then, *as* workers together *with him*, beseech *you*
also that ye receive not the grace of God in vain" (2 Corinthians 6:1). The
phrase "in vain" means "having no real value, worthless, not successful."
When Jesus was teaching, he referred to a group of people who claimed
they were working in their spiritual gifts under his authority, but Jesus denied them as his followers (Matthew 7:21-23). Now, if the physical church
has rules, regulations, and traditions that have to be abided by, how about
the Kingdom of God? Do not be mistaken—church organizations and
going to church are good things. Jesus set the structure of the church
organization himself. He is the head of the church (Ephesians 5:23). A

Godly church submits to the rules of Christ. The Bible points out specific behaviors that will not be tolerated in the Kingdom of God. Avoiding and eliminating these behaviors are necessary for Christians now and forever.

> Now the works of the flesh are manifest, which are *these*; Adultery, fornication, uncleanness, lasciviousness, Idolatry, witchcraft, hatred, variance, emulations, wrath, strife, seditions, heresies, Envyings, murders, drunkenness, revellings, and such like: of the which I tell you before, as I have also told *you* in time past, that they which do such things shall not inherit the kingdom of God. But the fruit of the Spirit is love, joy, peace, longsuffering, gentleness, goodness, faith.

> (Galatians 5:19-22)

> For this ye know, that no whoremonger, nor unclean person, nor covetous man, who is an idolater, hath any inheritance in the kingdom of Christ and of God. (Ephesians 5:5)

> Know ye not that the unrighteous shall not inherit the kingdom of God? Be not deceived: neither fornicators, nor idolaters, nor adulterers, nor effeminate, nor abusers of themselves with mankind, Nor thieves, nor covetous, nor drunkards, nor revilers, nor extortioners, shall inherit the kingdom of God. And such were some of you: but ye are washed, but ye are sanctified, but ye are justified in the name of the Lord Jesus, and by the Spirit of our God. (1 Corinthians 6:9-11)

> For if we sin wilfully after that we have received the knowledge of the truth, there remaineth no more sacrifice for sins. (Hebrews 10:26)

These sinful behaviors are a yoke of sin around the believer's neck. Lamentations 1:14 clarifies the point. It reads, "The yoke of my transgressions is bound by his hand: they are wreathed, *and* come up upon my neck: he hath made my strength to fall, the Lord hath delivered me into *their* hands, *from whom* I am not able to rise up." A yoke is "a device for joining a pair of draft animals." It immobilizes a person, takes away one's freedom, and causes stagnation. However, God has given his people a way out of the yoke of sin. It is a five-step program.

> If my people, which are called by my name, shall humble themselves, and pray, and seek my face, and turn from their wicked ways; then will I hear from heaven, and will forgive their sin, and will heal their land.
>
> (2 Chronicles 7:14)

All five steps in the repentance process are very important. Step one, "If my people" a person who admits and believes that God exists and is the Creator of the universe, also decides to accept God as the Lord of their life. "But without faith it is impossible to please him: for he that cometh to God must believe that he is, and that he is a rewarder of them that diligently seek him" (Hebrews 11:6). Step two, "humble" Barak, truly sorry for wrongdoing or thinking to the point of wanting (seeking) a change. Step three, "pray" talking and asking God for forgiveness, asking God for help. Step four, "seek my face" learning more of God's ways through the Holy Bible and applies His principles and laws to your personal situations. Step five, "turn" to leaves the sinful nature 100%, accepts God's answer at all cost, and actively obedience. The turn is only 180 degrees, the total opposite of the sin that the person was yoked to.

A person can be yoked into slavery or sin again.

Stand fast therefore in the liberty wherewith Christ hath made us free, and be not entangled again with the yoke of bondage. (Galatians 5:1)

A person can have both church membership and kingdomship simultaneously. Be careful that your praise and worship will not be counted in vain in God eyes. Between membership and kingdomship, which one is more important? Kingdomship is more important than membership. "But seek ye first the kingdom of God, and his righteousness; and all these things shall be added unto you" (Matthew 6:33). Be Blessed.

About the Author

Doris Jean Sanders was born and raised in Chicago, Illinois, as the youngest of nine children. She graduated from the University of Wisconsin–Milwaukee, and has worked as a registered nurse for twenty-four years.

Sanders is married and the mother of one daughter.

List of Reference

Comfort, Philip, & Elwell, Walter A. (2004). The Complete Book of Who's Who in the Bible. Wheaton, IL: Tyndale House Publishers, Inc.

Fruga, Alvin & Sennola. (Speaker). (1999). A Household of Worship. (Cassette Recording 40099102A). Tulsa, OK: Higher Dimensions Ministries.

Levey, Judith (Ed.). (1989). MacMillan Dictionary: For Children. New York: Simon & Schuster.

Lockyer, Herbert. (1967). All the Women of the Bible. Grand Rapids, MI: Zondervan.

MacArthur, John. (2005). Unleashing God's Truth, One Verse At A Time: The MacArthur Bible Commentary. Nashville, Tennessee: Thomas Nelson, Inc.

Meeks, James T. (Speaker). (1996). Do You Know How Valuable You Are? (Cassette Recording BA96059). Chicago, IL: Salem Baptist Church.

Meeks, James T. (Speaker). (1997). Do You Really Understand Praise. (Cassette Recording SA97041). Chicago, IL: Salem Baptist Church.

Meeks, James T. (Speaker). (1997). Do You Understand Praise part 2. (Cassette Recording BA97040). Chicago, IL: Salem Baptist Church.

Meeks, James T. (Speaker). (1998). How Does God Feel About Church. (Cassette Recording 032298A). Chicago, IL: Salem Baptist Church.

Meeks, James T. (Speaker). (1996). Is the Bridge Out. (Cassette Recording SB96006). Chicago, IL: Salem Baptist Church.

Meeks, James T. (Speaker). (1996). Things Go Better With Praise. (Cassette Recording BA96023). Chicago, IL: Salem Baptist Church.

Meeks, James T. (Speaker). (1996). Unlocking the Mystery of Praise. (Cassette Recording BA96021). Chicago, IL: Salem Baptist Church.

Munroe, Myles. (2000). The Purpose and Power of Praise& Worship. Shippensburg, PA: Destiny Image Publishers, Inc.

Webster's New Universal Unabridged Dictionary. (1996). New York: Barnes & Noble.